"One of the great dangers the church faces is moving into the future without being firmly anchored in the past. It is essential that as we look forward we also look back, and for this reason I'm especially thankful for Stephen Nichols. He has deep knowledge, a skilled pen, and a contagious enthusiasm. I highly recommend his book and the podcast from which it originated."

—TIM CHALLIES
Blogger
Challies.com

"The history of the church needs to be taught in various ways, and the form of this book—pithy stories and their lessons, what Stephen Nichols calls 'postcards'—is ideal for many who find themselves too busy to read larger chunks of text. Dr. Nichols is a master of this method, having honed his skill in composing these pieces for his podcast. Ideal for all who love church history—busy and not so busy."

—DR. MICHAEL A.G. HAYKIN
Chair and professor of church history
The Southern Baptist Theological Seminary, Louisville, Ky.

5MINUTES
in CHURCH HISTORY

An Introduction to the Stories of God's Faithfulness
in the History of the Church

STEPHEN J. NICHOLS

Ʀ *Reformation Trust*   A DIVISION OF LIGONIER MINISTRIES, ORLANDO, FL

5 Minutes in Church History
© 2019 by Stephen J. Nichols

Published by Reformation Trust Publishing
a division of Ligonier Ministries
421 Ligonier Court, Sanford, FL 32771
Ligonier.org   ReformationTrust.com

Printed in Ann Arbor, Michigan
Cushing-Malloy, Inc.
0000619
First Printing (USA)

ISBN 978-1-64289-131-7 (Paperback)
ISBN 978-1-64289-132-4 (ePub)
ISBN 978-1-64289-133-1 (Kindle)

Cover design: Ligonier Creative
Interior design and typeset: Katherine Lloyd, The DESK

Unless otherwise noted, Scripture quotations are from the ESV® Bible (The Holy Bible, English Standard Version®), copyright © 2001 by Crossway, a publishing ministry of Good News Publishers. Used by permission. All rights reserved.

Library of Congress Cataloging-in-Publication Data

Names: Nichols, Stephen J., 1970- author.
Title: 5 minutes in church history / Stephen J. Nichols.
Other titles: Five minutes in church history
Description: Orlando : Reformation Trust, 2019.
Identifiers: LCCN 2018039050| ISBN 9781642891317 (pbk.) | ISBN
    781642891331 (mobi)
Subjects: LCSH: Church history--Miscellanea.
Classification: LCC BR145.3 .N53 2019 | DDC 270--dc23
LC record available at https://lccn.loc.gov/2018039050

CONTENTS

PREFACE

This book offers a series of postcards from church history. There are postcards of people, places, events, artifacts, dates, and ideas. I offer these postcards in the hopes that you will enjoy visiting the past—and that you will go back there often.

These chapters were originally episodes on the podcast *5 Minutes in Church History*. The first episode aired on August 14, 2013. The three hundredth episode was released on September 26, 2018, as the podcast reached the five-year mark. This podcast is made possible by Ligonier Ministries, and many staff at Ligonier have contributed to the effort. These include Nathan Bingham, John Cobb, Dave Finnamore, Kevin D. Gardner, Caleb Gorton, Tyler Kenney, Kent Madison, Dirk Naves, Anthony Salangsang, and Dave Theriault. The whole thing started as a conversation with Chris Larson sometime in March 2013. I am grateful to all these and more at Ligonier. I am also grateful to the listeners. Thank you for spending five minutes with me each week. Finally, I am grateful to Megan Taylor for her efforts in helping me turn these episodes into chapters and into a book.

1

IS SPURGEON RIGHT?

The bombing of Britain during World War II leveled most of the area known as "Elephant & Castle" in the city of London. A row of pillars stood defiantly among the piles of rubble. These pillars belonged to the Metropolitan Tabernacle, the church that housed the larger-than-life preacher of the nineteenth century, Charles Haddon Spurgeon. Those pillars well represent Spurgeon. He was solid. He stood tall in his own day, and like the pillars, his legacy still stands.

Spurgeon has friends across many pews. Baptists like Spurgeon because he was a Baptist. Presbyterians like Spurgeon because he was so Reformed. Even Lutherans like Spurgeon because he was very nearly a nineteenth-century version of Martin Luther.

While Spurgeon held forth at the Metropolitan Tabernacle, Londoners would flock to hear him preach. In fact, people even traveled the Atlantic to hear him preach. He wrote many sermons, of course, while he was at the Metropolitan Tabernacle. And Spurgeon also wrote many books.

In one of his many books, Spurgeon made a comment well worth hearing. It comes from the preface to his book on commentaries. He had written this book to convince pastors of the need to use commentaries and to engage in deep study for their sermon preparation. Spurgeon well knew the value of reading for preaching. He had a personal library of around twenty-five thousand books. And this was in the 1800s. What's more, he actually read most of them.

In the preface to this book, he speaks to an objection to using commentaries. The objection goes something like this: As a Christian, I have the Holy Spirit. I have the Spirit's wonderful work of illumination. I don't need commentaries; I don't need to rely on the thoughts of others. I can go right to the source.

To that objection, Spurgeon replied, "It seems odd, that certain men who talk so much of what the Holy Spirit reveals to themselves, should think so little of what he has revealed to others."[1]

Spurgeon reminds us that the Holy Spirit is not an individual gift. The Holy Spirit is a corporate gift to the body of Christ. The Holy Spirit has taught others, and the Spirit uses others to teach us. Spurgeon's argument reaches the conclusion that preachers should use commentaries. Don't be arrogant, and don't think you have a corner on the market of the Holy Spirit, because you don't.

But what if we were to expand Spurgeon's argument in order to apply it to the relationship of today's church to church history? Here's my paraphrase of Spurgeon's argument: "I find it odd that the church of the 21st century thinks so highly of what the Holy Spirit has taught it today that it thinks so little of what the Holy Spirit taught the church in the first century, the second, the third, the fourth, and so on, and so on."

The Holy Spirit is not unique to our age. The Holy Spirit has been at work in the church for the past twenty centuries. We could put the matter this way—it is rather prideful to think that we have nothing to learn from the past. And remember, pride is a sin. And also remember, as Scripture says, "Pride goes before destruction, and a haughty spirit before a fall" (Prov. 16:18). We need a little humility. Enough humility to say we may not have all the answers in the present. Enough humility to say we need the past, and enough humility to visit it from time to time.

As Deuteronomy 6:10–11 vividly portrays for us, we drink at wells we did not dig, we eat from vineyards we did not plant, and we live in cities we did not build. We need that dose of humility that reminds us how dependent we are on the past and how thankful we need to be for those who have gone before us and dug the wells, planted the vineyards, and built the cities.

The past enriches our lives in surprising ways. In our past, our family history, we see examples of faithful disciples. We can be encouraged and even inspired by their faithfulness. But, far more, we see examples of God's faithfulness to His people. How does Paul put it in 2 Corinthians 1:10? He declares: "He delivered us from such a deadly peril, and he will deliver us. On him we have set our hope that he will deliver us again."

The centuries of church history give us a litany of God's deliverances. God has done it before, many times and in many ways, and He can do it again. He will do it again. And in that, we find courage for today and for tomorrow.

In church history, we see men and women facing challenges not unlike the challenges before us today. We look back and we learn. We also learn from the mistakes and missteps of the past. And, though it is a cliché, learning can be fun. Family stories of the exploits of crazy uncles inform; they also entertain. It is the same with our history, our family story. Let's get started.

THE EARLY CHURCH

■

2

THE FIRST OF THE TWO DISCIPLES OF JOHN: IGNATIUS

We begin our journey through church history with a direct link to the pages of the New Testament. This link is the two disciples of John, the Beloved Disciple. These two disciples are Ignatius and Polycarp. Ignatius' name has something to do with lighting a fire: *ignite*. Polycarp's name literally means "many fish." No one should forget such memorable names. Beyond their names, they also lived remarkable lives as two of the most significant figures in the late first century and the second century.

Ignatius was Bishop of Antioch, a city that factors prominently in the New Testament. At the city of Antioch, the followers of *Christus* were first called Christians. And a generation or so later, Ignatius served as the bishop at this exact spot to the second generation of the first group of people called Christians. We are not sure when he was born. Some put the date as early as AD 35. We do know that Ignatius died a martyr's death around 110. He was martyred in Rome by the Emperor Trajan. On his way to Rome, Ignatius had the opportunity to visit various churches, and he even was able to write letters to these churches. We have some wonderful pieces of literature of the early church in these letters from Ignatius.

What makes Ignatius significant beyond the place where he served as bishop is the place where he was from. Ignatius was from the city of Ephesus, and as a young man he was actually discipled by the Apostle John.

Ignatius, a direct link back to the New Testament era and the original disciples, wrote these various letters to the church because there were some serious problems in the church. John writes about these exact same problems in his epistles. He warns the church that false teachers will surely come. These false teachers are going to be teaching, among other things, that Jesus did not truly come in the flesh; He only appeared to come in the flesh. Not only were they plaguing the churches in John's day, they continued to plague the churches in the 100s. Ignatius followed the steps of his mentor and, in most of his letters, he addressed these false teachers who were denying the humanity of Jesus Christ.

Ignatius often starts off the chapters of his epistles with a singular warning, and he even gives a threat to the those who listen to these false teachers. He tells them, in essense, "Stop your ears when you hear these false teachers!"[1] Ignatius does not want this false teaching even getting so much as a foothold in the church. As you read through his epistles, you find out why. You see, if Christ didn't truly come in the flesh, then He really wasn't born, He really didn't live, He really didn't die on the cross, and He really didn't rise again. If Christ did not really and truly come in the flesh, then there is no gospel.

In fact, at the end of one of his epistles, he goes on to say that he wants to guard this church beforehand from these false teachers, whom he calls "beasts in the shape of men."[2] He doesn't shrink back from harsh language here because the stakes are so high. You must not only turn away from these beasts in the shape of men; you must flee. Ignatius wants to make sure that false teaching gets no foothold whatsoever in the church. Ultimately, he longs for even the false teachers to see the truth of the gospel. He declares:

> Only you must pray for them, if by any means they may be brought to repentance. For if the Lord were in the body in appearance only, and were crucified in appearance only, then am I also bound in appearance only. And why have I also surrendered myself to death, to fire, to the sword, to the wild beasts? But I endure all things for Christ, not in appearance only, but in reality. That I may suffer together with Him, while He Himself inwardly, strengthens me; for of myself I have no such ability.[3]

It was all-important for Ignatius that Jesus be truly human. In His true humanity, Jesus identifies with us and our humanity. Ignatius had suffered persecution, and he would go on to suffer a martyr's death. He endured and persevered those things because of his sympathetic High Priest. Jesus really was born, and He faced all the temptations and limitations of being truly human. He really died, and He really rose again. Make no mistake about it—Jesus came in the flesh. That was the message of John the Apostle, and that was also the message of John's disciple Ignatius of Ephesus, bishop of Antioch.

Trajan came to power in 98 and ruled over Rome until 117. He was a rather successful military leader and capable administrator. By most accounts, he was one of Rome's finest emperors. Around 110, he engaged in correspondence with Pliny, governor of Asia Minor at the time. Pliny wanted imperial advice on how to handle this new sect of Christians. Among the advice that Trajan offered is this comment: "If [Christians] are denounced and proved guilty, they are to be punished, with this reservation, that whoever denies that he is a Christian and really proves it—that is, by worshiping our gods—even though he was under suspicion in the past, shall obtain pardon through repentance."[4] How ironic.

Some of those who appeared before Trajan would not compromise their faith and would not falter. Ignatius was one of them. He did not deny Christ but instead professed Him—and that before the emperor of all of Rome. Ignatius, bishop of Antioch and disciple of John, became one of the first martyrs of church history.

3

THE SECOND OF THE TWO DISCIPLES OF JOHN: POLYCARP

"For eighty-six years I have been his servant. How then can I blaspheme my King who saved me?"[1]

These words were spoken by John's second disciple, Polycarp. Polycarp was the bishop at the church at Smyrna, a city of significance in the New Testament. And Polycarp, like Ignatius of Antioch, was a disciple of John. Born around AD 70, Polycarp was far younger than Ignatius, so he was actually discipled by John and by Ignatius. In fact, we can see this line stretch even further. As John discipled Ignatius and Polycarp, Polycarp discipled Irenaeus. Irenaeus discipled Hippolytus—now there's a great name from the early church. And so on and so on. We have this great line stretching through the first two centuries of the church's life that goes immediately back to John and to Jesus and stretches on through the pages of church history.

We know of Polycarp through an epistle that circulated widely through the early church known as *The Martyrdom of*

Polycarp. At eighty-six years old, he was considered the enemy of the state. Caesar himself saw to it that Polycarp would be arrested and that he would be martyred. The arrest warrant was issued, and the soldiers were dispatched to chase down Polycarp. Polycarp fled, and at one moment he hid in an out-building on the grounds of a large estate. The Roman soldiers caught up with him, learned of his whereabouts, and in they charged. Those soldiers were told they were hunting down an enemy of the state. They were poised and ready, weapons drawn. They executed their plan and burst through the door. They found an eighty-six-year-old man huddled against a stack of hay bales.

Polycarp took one look at his captors. They had been tracking him for days, and they were hungry. Polycarp ordered the master of the estate to prepare these soldiers a meal. After their meal, the soldiers arrested him and hauled him away.

Polycarp was imprisoned, and the day finally came for Polycarp's martyrdom. He was positioned in front of the crowd in the amphitheater. The jeering mob sat on concrete benches in row upon row in the vast semicircle. And behind Polycarp were the Christians, shackled, emaciated, and bruised and battered from beatings.

Now Polycarp was ordered to turn around and say to the Christians, "Away with the atheists."[2] This would be his way of recanting the faith. By saying, "Away with the atheists," he would be distancing himself from the Christians.

This likely requires some explanation. The early Christians were accused of atheism because they denied the gods of the state. And specifically, they refused to take part in emperor worship.

But what follows next is one of the greatest ironies in all of church history.

Instead of turning to the Christians and saying, "Away with the atheists," Polycarp turns to face the great crowd in the amphitheater. With one grand sweeping gesture of an outstretched arm, he points up and down the rows all around the semicircle, declaring with all the strength his aged voice could muster, "Away with the atheists." Polycarp was martyred that day.

The Martyrdom of Polycarp refers to Polycarp's day of martyrdom as "a day of victory." Then it closes with these three sentences: "Polycarp was arrested by Herod when Philip was high priest during the proconsulship of Statius Quadratus. But while Jesus Christ was reigning as King forever—To him be glory, honor, majesty, and the eternal throne, from generation to generation."[3]

Polycarp knew that Rome and Caesar were mere shadows. He knew that Jesus Christ is Lord of the universe. Caesar is not lord. Jesus is Lord. Polycarp was willing to live and to die for his Lord and King.

4

LYON

Early in the 100s, a church was started in Lyon (pronounced *lee-on*) in what was then Roman Gaul and under the control of the Roman Empire. From the beginning of the church, the local officials persecuted Christians. They hoped to eradicate Christians in their city and so harassed and persecuted them. But their efforts were to no avail. The Christians remained and thrived. By the time of the 170s, the local officials in Lyon stepped up their efforts and held nothing back in efforts to stamp out Christianity.

The 170s were not a time of intense empire-wide persecution. Marcus Aurelius, the philosopher, was ruling the empire, and he had turned his attention away from persecuting Christians. The persecution at this time, consequently, became more sporadic and intermittent. The persecution of Christians that was occurring reflected the attitudes of the local officials toward Christ. And in Lyon, as mentioned, the local officials had run out of patience.

The early church historian Eusebius wrote down and preserved the record of the Christians at Lyon and of the persecution they faced in his informative and inspiring book *The History of the Church*. Of the challenges faced by the Christians at Lyon he writes, "First of all, they endured nobly the injuries heaped upon them by the populous—clamors and blows and draggings and robberies and stonings and imprisonments, and all the things which an infuriated mob delight in inflicting on enemies and adversaries."[1] Among this list of persecutions, Eusebius mentions robbings. When Christians would leave their home in order to gather in worship, their neighbors would literally go into their houses and ransack and rob them.

The crucial moment came in 177. The officials of the city rounded up all the Christians together as one lot of criminals. They jailed them and after a time brought them into the public coliseum. One by one, they called each Christian forward. The officials confronted them, demanding that they answer one question: "Are you a Christian?" As Eusebius records, before this jeering mob and before these power-wielding officials, the Christians confessed. They confessed to no great crime against the Roman emperor or against the Roman Empire. They confessed to no great crime against their neighbors. They simply confessed that they were Christians, that they were followers of Christ. For this, they were tossed back into prison. All of this was contrary to Roman law, even a mockery of law.

They were imprisoned for a few weeks and treated harshly. This was an attempt to get them to recant their faith, which would shame and discredit them. A few did recant, but the vast majority maintained their confession and their conviction.

And then the martyrdoms started. They would individually be brought forth to the arena. For the entertainment of the mob, they would be martyred. Eusebius tells us that there were forty-eight Christians in Lyon that were martyred.

Eusebius tells us what happens to them. At one point, he says, all the people of the town "raged like wild beasts" against the Christians.[2] He records a testimony from one of the imprisoned: "Even if they had before been moderate on account of friendship, they were now exceedingly furious and gnashed their teeth against us."[3]

Eusebius tells the story of one particular martyr there at Lyon named Blandina. She should be far more known than she is, and her story is worth remembering. Eusebius refers to her as a "noble athlete."[4] Paul challenges us to be a good athlete, to be one who endures the race and endures with perseverance. Blandina stood in the arena before the crowd of "raging beasts" and simply said, "I am a Christian."[5]

But that was not the end of the church at Lyon. The officials were not able to arrest all of the Christians. One in particular was a young presbyter, or elder, named Irenaeus. He took a message, a plea for help really, to Rome. He met with the church there and worked with them to present his plea for mercy and intervention to the emperor himself, the philosopher-caesar Marcus Aurelius. We have no evidence that Irenaeus was able to have an audience before Marcus Aurelius and no evidence that he was able to present their case. By the time he returned to Lyon, these forty-eight people, these members of the community that he worshipped alongside of, had all been martyred. Irenaeus simply stepped in and continued the church at Lyon. He would go on to be appointed bishop of Lyon. He wrote many books, including the influential *Against Heresies*. He made a strong case against the so-called Gnostic gospels, insisting that as there are but four directions, east, west, north and south, there are only four Gospels. Irenaeus, too, ended his life a martyr.

5

THE CATACOMBS

Under the city of Rome lies a vast system of catacombs. The ancient Romans built these catacombs because they simply didn't like death—they feared it and didn't want to think about it. They wanted to push death out onto the margins, even out of sight, so they buried their dead underground in the catacombs.

This underground maze of catacombs plays an interesting role in the history of Christianity. In the first few centuries after Christ, Christianity was at odds with the Roman Empire. As we have seen, Christians were marginalized, ostracized, and persecuted. Despite the opposition they faced, they found that they could worship freely in the catacombs. The Romans would not venture down in the catacombs. They would send slaves to dig out the catacombs and bury their dead. So, the Christians were relatively free to worship there. They even sometimes built seats into the walls of these catacombs. They also left behind paintings on the walls.

The paintings, mostly frescoes, depicted key events in the Gospels. Some are of the Last Supper. Others depict miracles, like the feeding of the five thousand. Some depict scenes from parables. Some depict the calming of the storm at sea by Jesus when he was with the disciples. Many have a depiction of Jesus flanked by the Greek letters A and Ω—alpha and omega, the beginning and the end.

One testimony to the practice of worshiping in the catacombs is the wonderful early Christian hymn called "O Gladsome Light":

> O gladsome light, O grace
> Of God the Father's face,
> The eternal splendor wearing;
> Celestial, holy, blest,
> Our Savior Jesus Christ,
> Joyful in thine appearing.

This early Christian hymn continues, "The day falls quiet and we see the evening light." Can you see it in your mind's eye? The Christians are gathering in the catacombs. They have a fire or they have torches to light the darkness of these cavernous spaces and tunnels; it is their "gladsome light." They gather around the light to worship together and to sing their hymns of praise.

After Christianity was legalized and as it spread through the empire, catacombs became not only a place where Christians could meet; they also became the place were Christians would bury their dead. We can learn about the lives of early Christians from the epitaphs that were left at a number of these catacombs. One of them simply says, "Here lies Quintilian, a man of God, a firm believer in the Trinity, who loved chastity and rejected the allurements of the world."[1]

Another epitaph belongs to someone named Domitilla. It says, "Who believed in Jesus Christ, together with the Father, the Son, and the Holy Spirit."[2] Many of these early catacomb epitaphs reference Christians' belief in the Trinity. It shows how important that doctrine was to the early church.

Another of these epitaphs reads, "Here I rest, free from all anxiety, what I awaited has happened, when the coming of Christ occurs I shall rise in peace."[3] This is a wonderful testimony to resting in Christ.

One of these epitaphs addresses the person directly. Her name was Aproniane, and she was only five years and five months old when she died. Her epitaph says, "Aproniane, you believed in God, you will live in Christ."[4] This is a beautiful testimony to the hope of our salvation and the eternal life that we have in Christ.

Another of these epitaphs reads, "Now that I have received divine grace I shall be welcomed in peace."[5] This particular text is preceded by the early Christian symbol of the fish. One last epitaph simply says, "This person was a servant of the Lord Jesus Christ."[6]

These epitaphs, paintings, and hymns provide a beautiful witness to the lives and beliefs of early Christians who took the Lord's Supper together, who prayed together, who confessed the Apostles' Creed together, and who sat under the teaching of God's Word. And there in the catacombs, they sang together as they gathered around the gladsome light.

6

CAESAREA MARITIMA

Caesarea Maritima is a city rich in history—biblical history and church history. Today it is a national park in Israel, but previously it was one of the most important cities in Judea. Herod the Great built his palace there, and in AD 6 it became the administrative capital for the Roman governors of Judea. Of course, the governors would often go up to Jerusalem to conduct business, but their palace of choice was Herod's palace at Caesarea Maritima. As the governor's main residence, it saw a lot of commercial and political activity, giving it great prominence.

Because of the historical importance of this city, archaeologists have spent a great deal of time there uncovering all the treasures Caesarea Maritima has to offer. One such treasure was found in 1961. Archaeologists discovered an artifact that came to be known as the Pilate Stone.

This stone has four lines etched into it, and it refers to a building that was built and dedicated by Pontius Pilate. The original Pilate Stone has been moved from Caesarea Maritima to a museum in Jerusalem. It is (to date) the only archaeological reference to Pontius Pilate. A very significant find, this stone corroborates the biblical account in witnessing to the existence of a ruler named Pontius Pilate. He was a low-level Roman bureaucrat, but he is mentioned in the Gospels and in the Apostles' Creed. His mention is a reminder that this Christian faith of ours is grounded in space and time by identifying the governor at the time of Jesus' arrest, trial, and crucifixion. And at Caesarea Maritima we have a stone with his name etched upon it.

Caesarea Maritima also played a role in the rest of the New Testament. Paul was in Caesarea many times. Its port provided a suitable launching point for Paul to set out on his missionary journeys. He also spent two years there as a prisoner (Acts 24:22–27). Paul came to know the city very well. Peter also knew this city. He baptized the Roman centurion Cornelius at Caesarea (Acts 10:1).

As we move into the pages of church history, the city remains significant. The church historian Eusebius was from Caesarea Maritima. In his book *The History of the Church*, Eusebius chronicles the exploits of the Roman emperor Diocletian, who launched an empire-wide persecution of Christians. Eusebius records that the jails were so full of Christians under Diocletian that it launched a crime spree. The officials were so concerned with arresting Christians that common criminals were literally getting away with murder under the reign of Diocletian.

One of the victims of Diocletian's persecution was Pamphilus of Caesarea Maritima. Pamphilus, a Christian, was a significant figure in the life of the city and gets credited for building up the city's library. It was one of the best libraries in the ancient world. It is estimated that at one time it held more than thirty thousand manuscripts. It attracted scholars in all fields from across the empire. Theologians and early church leaders also made pilgrimages to study at Caesarea Maritima. Jerome, the translator of the Vulgate, the Latin translation of the Bible, spent time looking at the manuscripts, researching, and writing at Caesarea Maritima. Some other significant church figures, such as Gregory Nazianzus and Basil the Great, also spent time there, so great was its library and prominence as a center of study.

This city by the sea played a significant role in the New Testament and is one of the key places in church history.

7

325

Historians love dates—birthdays, anniversaries. They love to celebrate dates not simply for the sake of celebrating, but because dates represent events, real events in the lives of real people, when real, significant things happened. Dates represent *moments*, and those moments can help us understand our own lives.

One of the very important dates from the early church is not a birth or martyrdom date. It is the date of a church council held at the summer palace of Constantine in Nicaea in 325. Only a few decades before the Council of Nicaea, Christianity was illegal in the Roman Empire. In fact, the 290s and 300s were an intense time of persecution, almost an unprecedented time of persecution for Christians. Then came Constantine, and his so-called conversion—whether he truly converted is another question, but historians nevertheless speak of his "conversion." In the wake of that conversion, he issued the Edict of Milan in 313, which legalized Christianity. Constantine issued a few more edicts, and Christianity was no longer an illegal religion, or, as the Romans called it, an "illegal superstition."[1] Christianity was now legal.

Not only that, but Constantine also passed legislation that tended to favor churches and Christians, and within a generation, there was a massive spread of Christianity within the Roman Empire. One of those laws gave tax exemptions to church property. So, that brings us to the year 313. Just a dozen years later the Council of Nicaea was held in 325.

This was the first great ecumenical council. Meaning, representatives from all over the church were present to discuss matters of theological and practical urgency. The council was called because of one man—a presbyter, or elder, named Arius. He had promoted the idea that Jesus is unique—that Jesus is beyond us human beings—but that He's not God. And, of course, this gets right at the heart of orthodoxy: the statement that Jesus is the God-man. Arius' teachings were very disruptive within the early church. The bishops therefore came together to settle the matter for the church. Nicaea is a picture-postcard city. Today, the city is called Iznik. It's just off of Lake Iznik in Turkey. Constantine had a summer palace there. He invited all of these theologians to gather there in order to spend time working through these theological disputes, and the result was the Nicene Creed. In addressing this controversy, the council also gave us one of the best lines in theological literature. It is this simple line: "For us and for our salvation." Jesus is the God-man. His equality with God, as Paul tells us, is something that He did not have to grasp; rather, He *had* it already. Yet He took on flesh, incarnate. He was made human. He became one of us. He didn't simply appear to be human; He was human. He is the God-man. And He is the God-man for us and for our salvation. All of this provides good reason to celebrate the year 325.

8

WHAT A MOSAIC CAN TEACH US: HINTON ST. MARY, DORSET

England is a great place to visit during the Reformation, or even during the Middle Ages. Roman Britain also makes for a great place to visit to learn of the church in the early centuries. Let's go back to Roman Britain in the 300s, to the county of Dorset and to a charmingly named place: Hinton St. Mary. Actually, we need to go to London, to the British Museum, because it is there in that massive treasury of antiquity, in the early Britain room, that we will find a mosaic—the Hinton St. Mary Mosaic.

Archaeologists unearthed this mosaic in 1963. The full mosaic measures seventeen feet by fifteen feet. It was removed from Hinton St. Mary and taken to the British Museum in London. A "roundel," a circular mosaic, dominates the middle. This particular roundel features what is believed to be the earliest extant image of Christ. And it is flanked by the ancient Christian symbol of the Chi-Rho, two Greek letters that are the first two letters of Christ's name. (Three in English, because the Chi, which is the "X" in Greek, is transliterated as "Ch" in English, and the Rho is the "R.") This symbol goes back to Constantine.

Historians aren't sure of the purpose of the original building that housed this mosaic. Some think it was the dining room of a villa. Others think it may have been a church. We are not exactly sure what the room was used for. But here's the significance—Christ is the center of the mosaic. In art terms, we would say the focal point. Traditionally, a pagan god or a goddess would hold that place in Roman mosaics. And the four corners of the Hinton St. Mary Mosaic are given to the four Gospel writers. Typical Roman mosaics had the four winds or the four elements.

These Roman mosaics offer a sense of the Roman worldview, of how they saw the world and how they understood their world. Pagan gods were at the center. Nature was at the gods' command. And humanity was trying to figure it all out. Like Odysseus, humans are tossed about by the whim and capricious moods of the gods. That's one worldview.

Then there's another worldview represented in the Hinton St. Mary Mosaic. In this worldview, Christ is at the center and God's Word governs us, teaches us. God's Word, as represented in the four Gospels, leads us and points us to the center; it leads us and points us to Christ. When the craftsmen made this mosaic and shifted the paradigm from the Roman pantheon to Christ, it was akin to saying, "There's a new sheriff in town." And now, everything has changed.

If you were to visit the British Museum and walk around the early Britain room you would notice something rather quickly.

You would notice that the Chi-Rho symbol that appears on the Hinton St. Mary Mosaic is nearly ubiquitous. And so is another pair of Greek letters. These are the first and the last letters of the Greek alphabet—alpha and omega. We know these from the book of Revelation and the reference to Christ as the Alpha and Omega, the beginning and the end. As the beginning and the end, Christ also fills and dominates the middle.

One very fascinating artifact, or artifacts, in the British Museum with the alpha and omega is a pair of large copper basins from the fourth or fifth century. These have the alpha and omega hammered from the inside out, but the alpha and omega are reversed. We should muster a great deal of sympathy for the craftsman. If you are hammering letters into copper, you can't exactly hit the delete button and correct your mistake. So, there it is for all the ages to see, the omega and alpha.

All of these artifacts point to the rapid spread of Christianity after Constantine in the 300s and 400s. This rapid spread went across the English Channel and on up into ancient Britain. These artifacts and their symbolism remind us that Christ is at the center. Christ is the beginning and He is the end. He is even the end and the beginning. As Paul says in 1 Corinthians 8:6, "There is . . . one Lord, Jesus Christ, through whom are all things and through whom we exist."

9

AUGUSTINE'S BIG WORD

Navel-gazing refers to the excessive focus and concentration on the self. Call it "the belly button generation." Like infants who have just discovered their belly buttons, we are captivated by ourselves. It might be OK for infants to not be much aware of the world beyond their own selves, but as we grow up we need to see that there's a world around us, or we will lead rather shallow lives. At some point, we must outgrow our fascination with ourselves. This is yet another reason to study church history. We need to know that we are not the center of the universe. More importantly, we need to be reminded of what matters most. In this regard, we can receive guidance from one of the towering figures in church history: Augustine of Hippo.

Augustine was a convert from North Africa who rose to be a bishop. He chronicled his journey toward faith in Christ in his classic book *The Confessions*. From the very first word of *The Confessions,* Augustine wants his readers to know what's important. The first word in the Latin is *magnus*. It is usually translated "great," and one recent translation refers to it as "vast."[1] Augustine uses the word to refer to God. This first word and the truth it represents control Augustine's great book. There is something and someone far greater than us. The Greatest, in fact. After Augustine calls God the Greatest, he refers to himself as a mere segment, a dot. Now that's perspective. Rather than starting with our own belly button, we start with eyes upward, enthralled and awed by the transcendent greatness, magnitude, and vastness of God.

The Confessions, some historians tell us, is the first true autobiography. Kings had written chronicles of their exploits and conquests, but Augustine wrote the first autobiography. But we would be wrong to assume that Augustine is the main character. That role belongs to God. God is the hound of heaven who relentlessly tracked Augustine down and drew him to Himself. God made Augustine—and God made us, too—for Himself. But we run the other way. Augustine ran all over the Roman Empire in his futile attempt to seek pleasure and meaning, to seek truth, justice, and beauty, in something, anything, other than God.

Our restless hearts propel us in the opposite direction. The first paragraph of *The Confessions* ends with these words: "You have made us for yourself and our hearts are restless [Latin *unquietam*], until they rest [Latin *pace*, "peace"] in you."[2] We are not at peace. But this God who made us desires to remake us. Augustine liked to call humanity "Adam's sinful lump."[3] And this Great Potter, the Magnus, pulls some clay from this lump and reshapes it. He redeems sinful hearts through the atoning blood of the sacrifice of the God-man on the cross. He gives us peace.

So Paul says in Romans 5:1: "Therefore, since we have been justified by faith, we have peace with God through our Lord Jesus Christ." Yes, this is a great God. The Greatest. Our very first word should be none other than Augustine's. Our reflex should be, "I am but a mere segment, a dot. And You, O God, are great." We need this perspective in the world today, as Christians have needed it through the centuries past. While we are in this world, with its mixed-up perspective that sees people as big and God as small, we can magnify the greatness of God in our hearts and minds.

The Confessions is more than an autobiography; it's even more than a classic text—perhaps the finest text in all of Christian history. Augustine's *Confessions* is a prayer before the One who alone is God. And it should be the prayer of us all.

THE MIDDLE AGES

∎

10

THE $14 MILLION BOOK

A $14 million book sounds expensive, right? Believe it or not, that's not the most expensive book of all time. That honor goes to Leonardo da Vinci's codex, a seventy-two-page notebook that sold for $30.8 million at auction; it was purchased by Bill Gates. There are other books that are pretty expensive too. In 1987, a Gutenberg Bible went up for auction at $5 million, and for $6 million you could purchase a first folio of Shakespeare. There have been some other medieval manuscripts that have gone for significant money. There was a text called *The Gospels of Henry the Lion.* Henry the Lion was the Duke of Saxony. He commissioned this particular edition of the Gospels; it was a very elaborate book with a very elaborate cover. He commissioned it for the altar at the Brunswick Cathedral in Germany. It's a twelfth-century manuscript of the four Gospels and it sold for $11 million.

But the book we're talking about is known as the St. Cuthbert Gospel. This is a book from the late seventh or early eighth century. It's a rather simple book. It's only five and a half inches by three and a half inches, and it has a stamped leather cover over a wooden board binding. Its pages are cord bound and its pages are vellum. Vellum was a bit of a technological advance over papyrus; it is the skin of animals—in this case, calfskin. Vellum is very durable and very smooth, and it provides a great surface for writing. Paper makers moved from vellum to rags, literally cotton rags. Today paper is made, mostly, from pulp. This particular text from the Middle Ages, with vellum pages, is a Gospel of John. It was found in 1104 inside the coffin of Cuthbert.

This raises two questions. First, who was Cuthbert? Second, why were people looking in his coffin? Cuthbert was a monk and also bishop in the Lindisfarne area of England, and he died in 687. He was buried at the monastery at Lindisfarne. When the Vikings came along, they took all sorts of things from Lindisfarne, including Cuthbert's coffin. It was finally returned and ended up being installed at the Durham Cathedral in 1104. His coffin was opened to ensure that his remains were still in there. When they looked in, tucked away inside was this little, future multimillion-dollar leather Gospel of John—the St. Cuthbert Gospel.

The book seems to have disappeared from that point. It was in personal hands until the 1700s, when it ended up in a Jesuit monastery in Belgium. In 2012, the British Library purchased it for £9 million, or $14 million. You can see the book at the British Library site. There is actually a CT scan of it on the site, and every single page is digitized.

The text is laid out in a single column, and it is very simple. The scribe was very careful. Occasionally, there is an adorned capital letter, and sometimes you will find a letter painted in red. It begins simply, "*In principio erat Verbum*"—"In the beginning was the Word." There are no chapter divisions, there are no verse numbers, there is no table of contents; it just starts right in and goes right through the Gospel of John. There are well-spaced margins, surrounding a clean, crisp text.

This text is Europe's oldest intact book, and so it reminds us of the beginning of book publishing, which of course at that time was done carefully by hand. But it also reminds us of the role that the Gospels have played. It also reminds us of the role that the Gospel of John has played in the history of the church.

So, there we have it—a $14 million book. What's most fascinating about that book, of course, is the content. On those vellum pages are not simply words of value. There are words of eternal value.

11

CANTERBURY

There is perhaps no city more charming than Canterbury, England. The ancient cathedral city has played a prominent role in church history. So let's go on a field trip to Canterbury.

When the Romans arrived in the middle of the first century AD, they found an already thriving village. They set about doing what the Romans did: they built a little city of Rome. It was built on the high ground along the River Stour. They built a forum, they built temples to their gods, and they even built a theater. This little Roman city lasted until the collapse of the Roman Empire around 410.

Upon the collapse of the Roman Empire, the Roman army simply left. This left the town in a bit of disrepair. But about a century and a half later came Augustine. This is not Augustine of Hippo, author of *The Confessions* and *The City of God*, but the other one, the Benedictine monk and missionary. While there were small bands of Christians in England before Augustine arrived, he was able to organize them together and saw Christianity grow and expand.

Augustine was sent as a missionary to the Kingdom of Kent in modern-day southeast England, where Canterbury is located. Æthelberht was king of Kent; while he was a pagan, his wife, Bertha, was a Christian. She gave significant support to Augustine and brought him to the attention of her husband. Æthelberht was later baptized by Augustine and gave Augustine significant land and resources. On the land that Æthelberht gave him, Augustine built a monastery and also began work on what would become Canterbury Cathedral. Augustine was the first archbishop of Canterbury. By 597, the monastery was thriving. As an education center, it was essentially a university.

Over the next four centuries, of course, much happened in Canterbury, including the raids of the Vikings upon Great Britain and upon this charming city. Skipping ahead to 1066, we come to the Norman invasion of England, led by Duke William II of Normandy, known as William the Conqueror. Along with William came Lanfranc, who had been the abbot at the monastery at Bec and whom William installed as archbishop of Canterbury. When Lanfranc died, he was succeeded by Anselm of Canterbury.

Anselm penned some wonderful works. He wrote the *Proslogion*, in which we have the ontological argument for the existence of God, and *Cur Deus homo*, which addressed Christ's identity as the God-man. He began to focus the church's attention on the substitutionary atonement of Christ.

After Anselm, another famous archbishop was Thomas Becket. Becket was at odds with King Henry II, and in order to bring peace to the land, Becket put himself into self-imposed exile and left Canterbury. Later, Becket came back to Canterbury.

Henry dispatched four knights to find him. When they found him, these knights murdered him at the cathedral. T.S. Eliot dramatized the whole event in his twentieth-century play *Murder in the Cathedral*.

In the late 1300s, Geoffrey Chaucer wrote his famous *Canterbury Tales*. By this time, Canterbury was a prominent pilgrimage site, thanks to the shrine to Thomas Becket. In the prologue, Chaucer speaks of pilgrims making their journey during the springtime, and Chaucer then tells us:

> Then do folk long to go on pilgrimage,
> And palmers to go seeking out strange strands,
> To distant shrines well known in sundry lands.
> And specially from every shire's end
> Of England they to Canterbury wend.[1]

Such is the draw of this charming and storied city.

12

TRENDING IN
THE TENTH CENTURY

We seem to be obsessed with what's trending *now*. We need to keep our social media feeds and news feeds handy, within the reach of the swipe of a thumb. Of all that is happening, it's helpful to see what's rising to the surface and what is of significance. Rather than look at what's trending in the current hour or even in the current five minutes, let's look at what was trending for a century. To be specific, what was trending in the tenth century? What big movements or big ideas dominated the discussion and left their mark?

You could probably make a case for any number of things, but I want to talk about Cluny. Cluny was a monastery in France. Early in the tenth century, the leaders who established that monastery saw it as a place of significant reform for the church.

By the tenth century, the church had seen marked cultural decline. The previous century saw the Vikings roaming and pillaging and destroying virtually everything they could. Toward the end of that century, many of those Norse leaders converted to Christianity and settled down, but there remained the wake of the carnage that had been inflicted. The tenth century was also a time of spiritual upheaval, as the papacy was entering into a period of even more intense decline.

And so the monastery at Cluny was established to get the church back on track and as a movement of reform. Among the many leaders at Cluny, one stands out: Odo. His tenure at Cluny ran from 927 to 942. He stressed a return to the Benedictine rule, which brought an intense structure with an emphasis on work and prayer to monastic life. He also focused on worship and introduced significant art into the structures of churches in the tenth century. He realized that many people were illiterate. He hoped the art could inform and teach, as well as aid in worship. He was also very much committed to the idea of beauty and to bringing objects of beauty, expertly crafted and made, into worship.

The influence of the monastery at Cluny spread throughout the land, and over the next two centuries, one thousand monastic houses were established from the leadership at Cluny. Clearly, one of the significant factors and movements that trended in the tenth century was the monastery at Cluny.

We should also note two honorable mentions. One comes near the very end of the tenth century, and that is the baptism of Vladimir the Great, the grand prince of Kiev. Vladimir was baptized in 988. Christianity had come to Russia in the early 900s but Vladimir was a committed pagan, and he has a colorful history. His brothers were involved in killing each other so that they could take over the throne. In the wake of all that, Vladimir fled to Scandinavia, but then he was able to return, and he assumed his role as grand prince of Kiev from 980 to 1015. And he needed to settle on a religion. He sent his counselors out to gather information on the religions of Islam, Judaism, and Christianity. Vladimir settled on Christianity, largely because of what was happening in Cluny and the emphasis on beauty. Vladimir was baptized in 988, and while much of Russia was already accepting Christianity, his baptism accelerated the acceptance of Christianity in the lands of Russia.

One final honorable mention is the year 1000. The coming of the new millennium spread a great deal of doom as the end of the world was assumed to be coming. It was a time of intense apocalyptic speculation. Many thought the world would come to an end at 1000. And that was the final trend of the tenth century.

13

1066: A GOOD YEAR
FOR A MONK

In 1066, William left Normandy and invaded England. In October 1066, he won success at the Battle of Hastings. On December 25, 1066, Christmas Day, William the Conqueror was crowned king of England at Westminster Abbey. The year 1066 proved to be a crucial year in the life of William.

It also, as it turns out, proved to be a crucial year for the history of England. And 1066 even turned out to be a crucial year in the life of a monk. This monk was born in 1033. His name is Anselm. And he made his way to the monastery at Bec in Normandy. There, he came under the training of the abbot of the monastery, Lanfranc. And Anselm deeply admired Lanfranc. And apparently so did William. After William became king, he made arrangements to have Lanfranc become archbishop of Canterbury, as mentioned back in chapter 11. And in Lanfranc's absence, Anselm became abbot of the monastery at Bec.

While at Bec, Anselm wrote some of the most brilliant texts

of the Middle Ages. He wrote the *Monologion* and the *Proslogion*. These are heavy-duty philosophical texts that argue for the existence of God. These were not very lengthy works, but they were weighty works. And then Lanfranc died. And once again, Anselm was tapped to replace him. Anselm made his way across the channel. He was installed as archbishop of Canterbury in 1093. This would be a post that he would hold until his death in 1109. Now his time as archbishop had its share of difficulties. He found himself between the proverbial rock and a hard place as the king of England—or, we should say, two different kings of England—found himself at odds with the pope. And during those times, Anselm was kicked out. He was exiled from his post and exiled out of England.

Anselm actually greatly enjoyed these times of exile. He was freed from all of his administrative duties, and he could once again apply his mind to his writing. It was during one of these exiles that he wrote one of the most remarkable texts of the Middle Ages, the text titled in Latin *Cur Deus homo*, which means in English, "Why the God-man?"

This text is actually a dialogue, a dialogue between Anselm and a man named Boso. In the course of the dialogue, Anselm is trying to get Boso to reckon with the crucial starting point. And the crucial starting point is the great weight of sin. Once we come to grips with the great weight of sin, that we in our humanity have offended a holy, infinite God, then we are realizing that we have a huge problem and there's nothing we can do about it. God is a just God; He just can't sweep this offense of sin under some cosmic rug. He can't act as if it never happened. So we are left with this huge problem of our sin, and there's nothing we can do about it. There exists a wide gulf between God and man, an inseparable gulf due to sin. And into that gulf enters the God-man.

You might have heard the following hymn lyrics, "He paid a debt he did not owe, and I owed a debt I could not pay."[1] That in many ways encapsulates the argument of *Cur Deus homo*. Jesus as God made an infinite sacrifice. In His deity, He is able to make a sacrifice that is worthy to pay for the offense of sin. But yet, in His humanity, He identifies with us, with the offending party. In the one person of Jesus, the God-man, we have the answer to the great weight of sin. We have the far greater weight of Jesus' active and passive obedience. His righteousness far surpasses our unrighteousness before God.

So Jesus as the God-man is our substitute for our sin and for our salvation. This is a wonderful book by Anselm, *Cur Deus homo*. We should all be thankful for this monk, Anselm, and even thankful for the year 1066.

14

THE FIVE WAYS
OF THOMAS AQUINAS

The Middle Ages were a rather unique time in the history of ideas. When you study church history in the Middle Ages and when you study philosophy in the Middle Ages, you are studying the exact same people, events, books, and ideas. That is not true of other eras. It's certainly not true of the twenty-first century. The Middle Ages were the time of Christendom, the bringing together of all things under the rubric and sphere of the church. So we have not two separate disciplines of theology and philosophy in the Middle Ages, we have them both intertwined. And much of the theological-philosophical discussion revolved around God, His communication to His creatures, and the revelation of His will. To use philosophical categories, we would say metaphysics, epistemology, and ethics.

The high point of this theological-philosophical conversation in the Middle Ages arguably comes in the 1200s in the life and work of Thomas Aquinas. Not only was Thomas the greatest of the medieval thinkers, but he may very well be one of the greatest thinkers of all time.

Now Thomas Aquinas worked on his magnum opus for decades—the *Summa Theologica*. The best way to translate this would be "The Highest," or "The Best of Theology." One way would even be to translate it, "The Most . . . ," and that might be a fitting description. This is a massive work that just goes on and on for volumes. And in fact it is technically unfinished. Thomas never quite finished it before his death. It's a work that is full of many ideas, but one of those ideas comes down to us, both in the history of Christianity and even in the history of philosophy. If you look at philosophy textbooks you would find references to this. And this we call "Thomas' Five Ways," or the five ways that the existence of God can be proven.

The first way he borrows from Aristotle. Aristotle spoke of an "unmoved mover."[1] Aristotle thought that of all of reality, one of the things you could know for certain is that there is motion. And in order for there to be motion, there had to be something that started motion. And for an argument that's a little intense, he said you can't just simply have motion going into eternity backwards—that is, if you look back in time, you can't have simply motion going all the way back into eternity. Because if that was the case, you'd never start if it went back *ad infinitum*, as the Latin says, "to infinity." You'd never start. But we know motion started. Why? Because we have present motion. So, based on the observation of motion, Aristotle posited the idea of an unmoved mover. And Thomas Aquinas comes along and says the unmoved mover is God. That's the first way.

The second way applies this logic of the unmoved mover to the concept of causes. In addition to observing motion in the world, we also observe cause and effect as a reality in the world. One of the ways you can see this very clearly is if we were to go play a game of pool or billiards. Every time you hit the cue ball, and it hits into another ball, the ball that the cue ball hits, moves. That is what we see as a cause and effect. The effect of the one ball moving is set in play by the cause of the cue ball hitting it. And the cue ball moving is set in play by the pool stick hitting the cue ball. And the cause of the pool stick hitting the cue ball is set into motion by the pool player who pushes the pool stick along. So we see cause and effect. Maybe you have seen a "Newton's cradle" on a desk? If you pull three of the balls suspended off to the side and send them back, three balls will go off in the other direction. When you eat a meal, someone prepared it. The meal is the effect; the preparing of the meal is the cause. Effects don't merely pop into existence without a cause, any more than a meal can simply appear out of nowhere. So it is with the universe. The universe is one great and grand effect. It must have a cause, a first cause. So we have the second way, which Thomas states as "God is the first cause."[2]

The third way has to do with the nature of being. Thomas tells us that there are contingent beings and there is a necessary being. Contingent beings are ones who are dependent upon something else for their existence. They are effects that need a cause. But for all these beings who are dependent upon something else for their existence, there needs to be something behind them that is independent, a being that receives nothing from another and nothing from outside of itself. That is a necessary being. Thomas says that necessary being is God.

Then we come to the fourth way. Thomas notes, "Look around and what we see as we observe reality is gradations of being."[3] There are things that are better, and there are things that are worse. In order to have better and worse, well, we need two categories. We need "the best" and we need "the worst." In other words, we need perfection. And so we need a perfect being behind these gradations of being that we see in reality. And again, that perfect being is God.

Well, that leads us to the fifth and last way, what Thomas calls the argument from design. All natural things are oriented toward a goal and a purpose. And where does that come about unless they are being guided along by an intelligent being who is a designer? And that intelligent being is God.

Thomas Aquinas works through these Five Ways in the opening pages of his massive work the *Summa Theologica*. He wants his readers to know that the existence of God can be demonstrated. It can be argued. He also wanted his readers to know why the existence of God should be argued for. Thomas referred to God as the *ens perfectissimus*, the most perfect being. As Thomas said, "God lacks not any excellence."[4] Instead, God is all excellence, and He is all excellence in abundance. Consequently, all existence and all things are from Him, through Him, and for Him.

15

THE CATHEDRAL

Could you imagine starting a building project that you know you will not finish in ten or twenty or even thirty years? It's almost impossible for us to even think like that. Now try this: imagine starting a building project that you will not see completed in your lifetime. You won't even see it completed in your children's lifetime. And you won't even see it completed in your grandchildren's lifetime. Imagine a building project that would take not decades, but centuries to finish. If you can imagine that, then welcome to the building of a medieval cathedral.

Westminster Abbey, the iconic cathedral near the Houses of Parliament and Big Ben along the River Thames in downtown London, stands as a great example. The cathedral, begun in 960, is still having finishes and additions in the twenty-first century.

Cathedrals were such grand edifices that they were literally centuries in the making, and they exhibited a variety of styles. There are Norman cathedrals and English cathedrals. Some of the cathedrals have flying buttresses that support the great height and, of course, the significant weight of the cathedrals. Others have vaulted ceilings. The famous King's College Chapel in Cambridge is one of the finest examples of the vaulted ceiling style. These are marvels of art and architecture.

These cathedrals also have many commonalities. We can speak of at least five shared elements and features of these cathedrals:

- the narthex,
- the nave,
- the aisle,
- the apse, and
- transepts.

First is the narthex or vestibule. This is the part of the cathedral into which you enter as you come from the outside world, before you enter the sanctuary. The narthex is a transitional space to prepare you for entering into worship. In most cathedrals, these tend to be darker spaces without windows.

As you walk into a cathedral, that long center aisle is called a nave. Some think that it was named for a ship, from the word *naval*, and it comes from the shape of a ship.

On each side of the nave are the aisles. The sides of the cathedral are considered the aisles.

At the far end, you have the apse. The apse is the semicircular, domed portion of a cathedral. There, you will find the pulpit or the altar. Usually, in the back of the apse, there are windows made of stained glass. And, since cathedrals are oriented to the east, as the sun rises, its rays penetrate that stained glass and flood the nave of the cathedral with light.

In front of the apse, the cathedral branches out to each side. These branches are called transepts. The word *transept* literally means "a partition across." The transepts on either side form two arms, as it were, that extend out from near the front of the cathedral. If you look at a cathedral from above, you very clearly see a cross shape.

As you walk into a cathedral, your eyes are drawn upward by the columns and the architecture. Even the geometrical shapes within the cathedrals draw your eyes upward; they lift you off this human horizontal plane and point you toward God. These medieval cathedrals are wonderful feats of architecture. They are cross-shaped and heaven-focused.

16

RAPHAEL:
STANZA DELLA SEGNATURA

The Renaissance artist Raphael (1483–1520) is considered one of the great masters of his day, and he is one of the most well-regarded artists of all time. Among his many famous works is the *Stanza della Segnatura*. This is not simply a single piece of art. The *Stanza* is actually an entire room. Raphael was commissioned to adorn this room, which functioned as a private office and library for Pope Julius II. The *Stanza* is the result. Not only is this room stunning art, but it well conveys the spirit of the Renaissance. The *Stanza* also helps us capture the pivotal time of transition from the end of the medieval era to the dawn of the Renaissance and the Reformation.

If you haven't heard of the *Stanza della Segnatura*, you may still have heard of the painting *The School of Athens*. It depicts the philosophers Plato and Aristotle, surrounded by other great Greek philosophers. Plato and Aristotle are each holding a book; Plato is holding the *Timaeus*, one of his dialogues, and

Aristotle is holding his *Ethics*. The choice of these two books as representative of these two figures is intentional. It was saying that Plato, and those who followed him, focused on questions of metaphysics, the big questions of being and of God. The *Timaeus* is a dialogue that argues for the existence of God. Plato is also portrayed with his index finger raised and pointed above, signifying the unity of all things and signifying that we must look to the heavens above for the crucial answers. Aristotle holding his *Ethics* is supposed to convey the idea that he, and those who followed him, were more interested in the question of how we live in this world. Aristotle is depicted with his hand spread out and pointing downward, signifying the diversity of things and signifying that we look to the natural realm for the answers. Such may be an oversimplification of these two great thinkers, but Raphael was nevertheless expressing this widely held view of the two different emphases of these two towering philosophers, Plato and Aristotle.

I remember first seeing a print of *The School of Athens* and immediately having the impression that this was simply a painting, framed and hanging on a museum wall somewhere in the world. But that's not what it is at all. In fact, it is a wall. Raphael actually painted it to fit the contours of the room. So it goes over the doorways and fits the curvature of the walls.

But there is even more to it than that, because this room has, like most rooms, four walls, and each wall is a painting. Exactly opposite *The School of Athens* is the *Disputation of the Holy Sacrament*. This painting has a number of biblical figures, and it's even laid out like a triangle, which many think hints at the Trinity. The painting includes figures from church history, including popes such as Gregory the Great. It includes Ambrose of Milan, who baptized Augustine; Augustine himself; and Jerome, who led the team of translators that produced the Vulgate, the Latin translation of the Bible. Raphael even includes some medieval figures such as Dante. This wall is a who's who of church leaders and theologians, just as *The School of Athens* offers a roll call of the great Greco-Roman pantheon of philosophers.

Disputation of the Holy Sacrament is a counterpart to *The School of Athens*—there is philosophy on one side of the room and theology on the other side. But that leaves two more walls. On one of the remaining two, Raphael painted representations of the arts and the sciences. He has various artists, musicians, and scientists. On the fourth wall, Raphael depicts the virtues and justice, representing ethics.

Do you see what Raphael is doing here? He is trying to present a worldview. This is more of a twentieth-century term, not one that Raphael would use, but he is presenting a comprehensive look that sees philosophy, theology, the arts, the sciences, and ethics as a unified whole. Of course, there are specialists in those fields, but in the *Stanza della Segnatura*, they are unified. They all form one room and one unified whole.

But a room also has a ceiling, and this, I think, is the key to the painting. The ceiling is actually a depiction of God in heaven. And God is handing out books to angels, who pass them along to the four walls. God hands a book to an angel, who then passes it on to the philosophers; and God hands a book to another angel, who passes it on to the theologians; and so on with the artists, the musicians, the scientists, and the mathematicians.

The idea is that God is the source, the unifier, of all things. In Raphael's delightful creation, we see God at the center as the revealer of all things, who holds all things together in the fields of theology, church life, philosophy, the arts, music, and all other virtuous pursuits. The room reminds us to look up, to look to God as the source of all wisdom, beauty, and virtue.

17

THE FIVE HUNDREDTH ANNIVERSARY OF 1516

The year 2017 marked the five hundredth anniversary of the start of the Protestant Reformation, when Martin Luther posted his Ninety-Five Theses on October 31, 1517. It is also worth noting that 2016 marked the five hundredth anniversary of 1516. That year set the stage for the immediate context of the start of the Reformation. A better understanding of that immediate context can only serve to deepen our appreciation of the monk with a mallet.

We can look at three things from the year 1516. The first is a painting called the *Haywain Triptych.* It was painted by the Dutch Renaissance painter Hieronymus Bosch. He was born in 1450 and died in 1516. This painting was one of his last major works.

A triptych is a painting with three panels. They were usually installed on altars. The two end panels would open and close, and painters would often paint the outside of these panels as well. On the outside of the *Haywain Triptych* is a painting that Bosch called *The Wayfarer.* It depicts a man who is trying to make his way through what is apparently a rather rough pilgrimage. He is being chased by dogs, and in the background you see another pilgrim being robbed and other people fighting. This panel is meant to show that things were not all that rosy in 1516. As you open the panels, you see that things get even worse. The left panel depicts creation; as you work your way down the panel, you see God creating Adam and Eve, and then you see Eve being tempted, and you know where that's going to lead. At the bottom of the panel, you see Adam and Eve being expelled from the garden. The far right panel depicts judgment and the torments of hell and final judgment.

The center panel is fascinating, and it is what gives the triptych its name. In the middle of the center panel is a haywain, or hay wagon, upon which there is a very large hay bale. And on top of this hay bale, curiously enough, is an angel that is pointing upward. In the sky is Christ, and He is looking down on a group of people. But none of the people are looking up—they are not noticing Christ at all. They are trying to pluck some hay off of the wagon. You see a number of people in the background who are obviously poor and destitute, and they are being kept from the hay. It's as if the nobility is keeping the masses away from these material benefits. And you also see, in the foreground, church officials who are enjoying an indulgent lifestyle. They are paying no attention to the masses of people in need, and they are paying no attention to Christ above. So, we go from creation and fall to judgment, and in between is redemption, but it was being missed at this moment in the church's history. So Bosch's *Haywain Triptych* portrays the great need of the people in 1516.

The second thing we could mention from 1516 is the Greek text. This, of course, is Erasmus' Greek New Testament. It was published in 1516 as the *Novum Instrumentum Omne.* It was actually a Greek text side by side with a Latin text, which was no easy feat to pull off with typesetting and printing, but that's what Erasmus did at Basel, Switzerland. It took him more than a year to complete. Erasmus' Greek text is important because it played a role in the Bible's once again returning to the center of church life. The Bible has the solution for all those people in Bosch's *Haywain Triptych* who are missing the solution to their ultimate problems in life.

The third thing we could mention from 1516 is that coffee was introduced to Europe from Arabia. So, 1516 tells us about our need through Bosch's *Haywain Triptych;* it gives us the Greek text, which would provide the solution; and it gives us coffee, which would provide fuel for the theologians as they engaged the text and engaged the pressing theological issues of the time.

That's 1516. The stage is set. All we need now is a courageous Augustinian monk who is ready to grab his mallet.

THE REFORMATION

■

18

FIVE THINGS AT ERFURT

The cathedral and university town of Erfurt in Germany helps us understand some of the formative moments in Martin Luther's life before he got to Wittenberg and before the posting of the Ninety-Five Theses. Luther was born in Eisleben—which will end up being the town in which he died. His family moved to Mansfeld shortly after his birth. Luther then went to Magdeburg for his first formal schooling. Next, he went to the school at Eisenach. This town, which sits in the shadow of Wartburg Castle, will later factor into Luther's life. This town was also the birthplace and longtime home of Johann Sebastian Bach. The school at Eisenach had two famous pupils: Luther and Bach. Both loved God and both loved music.

In Eisenach, young Martin established himself as a good student. He had to sing for his supper, so to speak. He'd be on the street corner singing, *Panum propter Deum*, "bread, for God's sake."[1] But he established himself as a scholar and later made his way to Erfurt.

Erfurt was quite the university town. The university was

established in 1392, and the town had many churches. There were twenty thousand people within the town walls when Luther was there in the early 1500s. In addition to its many churches, it also had a monastery. Let's look at five things about Luther at Erfurt.

The first is that Luther studied law. He earned his bachelor's degree in 1502 and his master's degree in 1505. That summer, he decided to visit his family in Mansfeld. On July 2, 1505, as he was returning to Erfurt, he was caught in a thunderstorm. Luther thought that God unleashed thunder from the skies to get him, to take his very soul. He cried out: "St. Anne, help me! I will become a monk,"[2] calling on the patron saint of miners. His father, Hans, made his living in the mines, supervising two of them. The family home had a shrine to Saint Anne. Luther likely stopped before the shrine to say his prayers to his family's patron saint as he headed out the door. It is no surprise at all that Luther would turn to Saint Anne for help when he needed help the most.

Luther survived the storm, finished his journey to Erfurt, and kept his vow. He turned over his law books to his friends and threw a party to say goodbye. In the middle of the night, he knocked on the door of the Augustinian monastery at Erfurt. Luther became a monk. This is the second thing to note about his time in Erfurt.

The third thing to know is what Luther would call "monkery." He was a very devout monk; he thought that through his monkery he could somehow attain righteousness. Later in his life, Luther reflected on his time in the monastery, recollecting, "If ever a monk got to heaven by his monkery, it was

I."[3] Luther poured himself into pleading his case before God. He would spend hours in the confessional. He would spend sleepless nights pleading his case before God. He skipped even the sparse meals of his fellow monks in order to somehow get closer to God. By his own testimony, however, all of his efforts at monkery never got him closer. In fact, as a monk, Luther felt more distant from God than at any other point in his life.

The fourth thing we need to know about Erfurt is that it was from here that Luther was sent on a pilgrimage to Rome. Johann von Staupitz, vicar general of the Augustinians in this region, was asked for advice on how to handle this overzealous monk. Staupitz said to send him to Rome because that would be great for his soul. When Luther arrived at Rome, he was utterly disillusioned by nearly everything he saw. Upon climbing the *Scala Sancta* or Holy Stairs, an act for which pilgrims earned a plenary indulgence, he uttered the famous words, "Who knows if it is true?"[4] Luther was looking to his church for something, and instead he found disillusionment.

The fifth thing, and maybe the most important thing, about Erfurt was that Luther was exposed to the Bible there. It was in the library in the Augustinian monastery that Luther held a complete Bible in his hands for the first time. And it was there that Luther lectured on the Bible for the first time. He later transferred to the Augustinian monastery in Wittenberg and began lecturing on the Psalms and on Romans, Galatians, and Hebrews. You don't have to spend much time in those books to recognize that the salvation that Luther was seeking can be found in them.

19

REPENT!

They are probably the most famous doors in church history. They might even be the most famous doors in history. They are the doors of the *Schlosskirche*, the Castle Church, in Wittenberg, Germany. The doors that exist now are not the original wooden doors to which Martin Luther nailed the Ninety-Five Theses. Those doors are long since gone, having burned in 1760; they have been replaced by bronze doors. The bronze doors are very heavy; they weigh over a ton. Inscribed on the doors are the Ninety-Five Theses in Latin.

When he posted the theses, Luther was very troubled by what was happening in his church. Two events were troubling Luther, and they converged in October of 1517. The first was an indulgence sale carried out by the monk Tetzel on behalf of Albrecht, archbishop of Magdeburg and an elector of Mainz. (In 1518, he would become a cardinal.) Albrecht had struck a deal with Pope Leo X. Leo X had bankrupted the church's treasury in his efforts to build St. Peter's Basilica. Having

Michelangelo paint the Sistine Chapel ceiling, among many other things, came with a steep price tag.

Albrecht needed a papal dispensation for him to take on additional bishoprics. To finance the whole deal, Leo X gave his papal imprimatur to an unprecedented indulgence sale. Tetzel stepped in, devised a scheme to sell them, and peddled the pieces of paper that promised forgiveness. Luther wrote letters to Albrecht over the summer of 1517 raising his objections.

The other event that troubled Luther was the coming unveiling of new relics acquired by Frederick the Wise. This was scheduled for November 1, 1517, All Saints' Day, or All Hallowed Day. October 31 is the evening before All Saints' Day, or Hallowed Evening, from which we get Halloween.

Luther could no longer keep silent about these abominable practices. In the preface to the Ninety-Five Theses, Luther wrote:

> Out of love for the truth and the desire to bring it to light, the following propositions will be discussed at Wittenberg over the oversight of the reverend father Martin Luther, master of arts and of sacred theology and lecturer on these subjects at Wittenberg. Wherefore, he requests that those who are unable to be present and debate orally with us may do so by letter. In the name of our Lord Jesus Christ, amen.[1]

And then he went on to present the Ninety-Five Theses.

Luther was calling for a debate. In his role as a priest, he saw himself as having an intense obligation concerning the eternal souls of those under his care. And as a theologian, he also had an obligation to the church to see that it maintained the truth and maintained orthodox teaching. As Luther studied the Bible and compared it to what he was seeing in the church, he saw a significant incompatibility, that there was a wide gulf between them. So, he called for a debate.

We can see in the first two theses what Luther was up to. In the first thesis, he wrote, "When our Lord and Master Jesus Christ said, 'Repent,' He intended that the entire life of believers should be repentance."[2] Now, it's fascinating that Luther would say that. In 1516, Desiderius Erasmus published his critical Greek New Testament with the Greek text on one side and the Latin text on the other side. A copy made its way to Wittenberg, and Luther read it. He poured himself into this Greek text, and he realized early on that the Latin text mistranslated Christ's first sermon, in which He says, "Repent." The Latin has *poenitentiam agite*, which translates to "do penance." Luther knew enough Greek to know that's not a good translation. In fact, he goes on to tell us in his second thesis, "The word 'repentance' cannot be understood to mean the sacrament of penance or the act of confession and satisfaction administered by the priests."[3]

So, the stage is set. On one hand, we have the biblical teaching. On the other hand, we have the teaching of the church. As Luther rolled through the Ninety-Five Theses, he continued to challenge the church. He was after the truth.

Luther stepped out of the Black Cloister, the Augustinian monastery in Wittenberg. He had the rolled-up theses in one hand, and he had a mallet in the other. As he passed through the gate, he turned left and walked two or so kilometers along the cobblestone street. He came to the Castle Church. In those days, there was a trellis and a wooden gate that led to a path that led to the church doors. He passed through the gate and stood in front of the doors. He held up to the church door the Ninety-Five Theses he had just written, steadied a nail, and swung the mallet.

20

MRS. LUTHER

Martin Luther gets a lot of attention, and rightly so, but we should not overlook Mrs. Luther—Katharina von Bora. In fact, looking at Katie offers quite a perspective on Martin Luther and the Reformation.

Katie was born on January 29, 1499. We don't know much about her early childhood. There's even dispute over the town she was born in. When she was around five years old, she was sent to a cloister for her education. By the time she was ten years old, she was at a monastery in the town of Nimbschen.

Sometime after Luther nailed the Ninety-Five Theses to the church door at Wittenberg, a friend of his named Leonard Kopp, a fish merchant, was delivering barrels of herring to the convent at Nimbschen in an effort to help nuns escape. Kopp arrived there late at night and unloaded his herring from the barrels, and then in the morning the nuns made their way into the back of his cart and hid behind the barrels. The tarp went over the barrels, and they drove off on his horse-drawn wagon. They ended up at Wittenberg, and Luther found husbands for many of these nuns among the students at Wittenberg. Luther sometimes quipped that he was used to start the Reformation just so he could become a marriage broker. But there was this one nun in particular, and none of the other suitors were quite good enough for Katie. She had her eyes on Luther himself. On June 13, 1525, Luther married her. And so this monk married a nun. The historian William Lazareth said, "Luther's marriage remains to this day the central evangelical symbol of the Reformation's liberation and transformation of Christian daily life."[1]

Before the Reformation, to be married was seen as being too concerned with temporal matters. Nuns, of course, were married to Christ, and priests were married to the church. And the Roman Catholic Church mandated clerical celibacy. But Luther, by marrying Katie, redeemed daily life and restored the institution of marriage to the rightful place that God had intended for it and that Scripture teaches us about it.

Katie was an early riser; Luther called her the "morning star of Wittenberg."[2] She would be up at 4 a.m., and she had plenty of things to keep her busy. She ran the family farm. At one point, she ran a brewery. Martin and Katie had six children, one of whom died in infancy. And there were a few more orphaned relatives whom the Luthers took in and raised. The house was always full of students and travelers.

When Martin died in 1546, Katie's life was difficult. War and the plague had racked Wittenberg. This affected their lands and their home. At one point, Katie had to flee the city, and she came back only to find that their farm was in utter ruin. Without her husband's income as a professor or pastor, she was in dire financial straits. She once wrote to a friend, "I find myself clinging to Christ like a burr to a dress."[3]

Perhaps there we learn a singular insight from the life and legacy of Luther. We see in Katie this emphasis on Christ, this clinging to Christ when all else is lost. We see there the essence of Luther's theology and the essence of the Reformation.

In 1552, the Black Plague came to Wittenberg and Katie had to flee. She went to the town of Torgau, and there, on December 20, 1552, Katie died. That is the life of Katie von Bora, Mrs. Luther.

21

TYNDALE'S ONLY
SURVIVING LETTER

There are many surviving books of William Tyndale. Of course, the most famous one is the Tyndale Bible. But in terms of material from his own hand, only a single letter survives. It is in Latin, and it was written while Tyndale was a prisoner at Vilvoorde Castle in Belgium, about six miles north of Brussels. The castle was built in 1374, and it had a lot of cold and dingy dungeons.

The life of Tyndale could easily be made into a movie. He was an outlaw. There are stories of friends betraying him, of last-minute escapes in the middle of the night. His was a life full of adventure as he stood against king and pope. And he spent his final years as a prisoner in a castle in that cold and dank dungeon. This circumstance of Tyndale will shed some light on this letter. Let's read it in full:

> I believe, right worshipful, that you are not ignorant of what has been determined concerning me. Therefore,

I entreat your lordship, and that by the Lord Jesus, that if I am to remain here during the winter, you will request the Commissary to be kind enough to send me from my goods which he has in his possession, a warmer cap, for I suffer extremely from cold in the head, being afflicted with a perpetual catarrh [inflammation in the nose or throat], which is considerably increased in the cell.

A warmer coat also, for that which I have is very thin: also a piece of cloth to patch my leggings; my overcoat is worn out; my shirts are also worn out. He has a woolen shirt of mine, if he will be kind enough to send it. I have also with him leggings of thicker cloth, for putting on above; he has also warmer night caps. I wish also his permission to have a lamp in the evening, for it is wearisome to sit alone in the dark.

But above all I entreat and beseech your clemency to be urgent with the Commissary that he may kindly permit me to have my Hebrew Bible, Hebrew Grammar, and Hebrew Dictionary, that I may spend my time with that study. And in return, may you obtain your dearest wish, provided it is always consistent with the salvation of your soul.

But if, before the close of the winter, a different decision be reached concerning me, I shall be patient, abiding the will of God to the glory of the grace of my Lord Jesus Christ, whose Spirit, I pray, may ever direct your heart. Amen.

W. Tyndale[1]

Just as Paul did in 2 Timothy, Tyndale asked for his cloak and for his books. Tyndale would spend his last days in the castle at Vilvoorde. He would be led from the castle and martyred on Friday, October 6, 1536. The accounts of Tyndale's martyrdom say that he was calm, and in fact, he said: "I call God to record that I have never altered, against the voice of my conscience, one syllable of His Word. Nor would do this day, if all the pleasures, honours, and riches of the earth might be given me."[2]

Tyndale faithfully served God throughout his life. He sacrificed much of his life as he was literally on the run as an outlaw trying to translate the Word of God into English so that his countrymen could have the Word of God in their native tongue. Even up until his death, he was faithful to his God.

It is very obvious, too, what Tyndale was thinking about. As he was led to his martyrdom, his final words were, "Lord, open the king of England's eyes."[3] There was no bitterness. He was not angry; he was not trying to get out of the charge. Instead, Tyndale was praying that God would open King Henry VIII's eyes so that he would see the truth of the gospel. Ultimately, Tyndale was praying for—and he labored for—the light of the gospel to shine across his native land of England.

22

HYMNS OF THE REFORMATION

Martin Luther once said, "Next to the Word of God, music deserves the highest praise."[1] Luther is of course well known as the composer of the beloved hymn "*Ein' feste Burg ist unser Gott*," or "A Mighty Fortress Is Our God." But this was not Luther's first hymn.

Luther wrote his first hymn in 1523. The context was that there were two monks from Antwerp who were summoned to Brussels and put on trial. They had expressed their devotion to the gospel, and there in Brussels they were condemned as heretics, excommunicated, and burned at the stake. When word of this event got to Luther, he decided to commemorate their lives and their martyrdom through a hymn. Luther titled it "A New Song Shall Here Be Begun." It's a folk ballad, really, and it's seventeen stanzas long.

After writing that song, Luther looked at the liturgy of the church and decided that the church needed an overhaul of its music just as it much as it needed an overhaul of its theology. So, he wrote a letter to George Spalatin, who was secretary to

Frederick the Wise and also a fellow preacher in Wittenberg. Luther wrote: "Grace and peace. I am planning, according to the examples of the prophets and the ancient fathers, to create vernacular psalms, that is hymns, for the common folk so that the Word of God remain with the people also through singing. Therefore, we are looking everywhere for poets."[2] Luther threw his effort into this hymn-writing project, and by 1524 the first hymnbook was produced. It had eight hymns, four of them by Luther. By 1546, there were more than one hundred hymnals printed.

In the next century, there would be hymns from the folks in the English-speaking church. But first were Luther and these German hymns. The most famous of his thirty-eight hymns is "A Mighty Fortress Is Our God." The title and first line conjure up the image of a castle, a stronghold, not unlike Wartburg Castle as it towers over the town of Eisenach, where Luther stayed after the Diet of Worms. Looking at the Wartburg, you get a sense of security. Luther wants us to think of God as our mighty fortress, as a bulwark who never fails us.

But there's another line that is worth considering from Luther's great hymn. A few stanzas in, Luther tells us, "That word"—that is, Christ, the Logos—is "above all earthly powers." This castle in Luther's day represented power; cannons were poised and ready to defend it. And yet Luther knows that above these earthly powers there is yet another power, and that is Christ, who is indeed above all earthly powers.

23

SIXTY-SEVEN WALLOONS

This is not the story of ninety-nine red balloons; this is the story of sixty-seven Walloons. Walloons are people from Wallonia, the southern half of Belgium. Wallonia is a French-speaking region. It has its own flag, its own anthem, and even its own Reformation confession. That confession, the Confession of the Walloons, was signed by forty-eight men, eighteen women, and one infant. That's sixty-seven Walloons.

At the time of the Reformation, Wallonia was actually part of northeastern France. Much like the rest of France, it was a place where the Reformation had difficulty in making its presence felt.

In 1522, in the city of Wesel, Wallonia, an Augustinian monk named Matthew Von Gingrich began introducing Lutheran ideas. By the 1540s, the city was captured by Lutheran and Reformation ideas and had a bit of a reputation as a city that would be friendly to the Reformation.

At the same time, there was another group of Walloons further south who were influenced less by Luther and the German

Reformation and more by Calvin and the Swiss Reformed church. They were persecuted by the local Roman Catholic authorities and petitioned the city council of Wesel to give them refuge. By trade, these were weavers and makers of textiles. The Wesel city council, in granting them refuge, provided a building for them, and they went there and set to work.

These Walloons were not only interested in textiles and weaving but also in theology. And so, they wrote a confession of faith, and on February 4, 1545, they presented it to the city council. It is not as long as many of the other confessions of the Reformation era, but it reflects the key ideas and theology of the Reformed Confessions. Let's take a look at a few excerpts.

The preface simply says, "The Confession of the Walloons, who have come into the city of Wesel on account of the gospel and to have a preacher in their own language and also to start on two lines the textile trade and the high-low warp loom."[1]

Then they go on to give their confession of faith. They declare, "We believe what is contained in the creed of the Apostles and of the council of Nicaea."[2] They affirm the true humanity and true deity of Jesus Christ. They affirm the Trinity. They go on to discuss the Lord's Supper, saying that it is not to be taken in just one kind—the Roman Catholic practice was to withhold the cup from the laity—but to be taken in both kinds, bread and wine.

They also had some fascinating other paragraphs to their confession of faith. They say, "Also concerning magistrates and the power of the sword, we feel and maintain that it is necessary to honor and obey the magistrates, not only the good and humble but the rude and wicked, as much and so long as they do not command anything against Christ."[3] These people were persecuted, so for them to say "honor the government" is significant. They go on to say, "This is why we reject and hold in execration all sects who are against the Word of God such as the Anabaptists, the Sacramentarians [Roman Catholics], and the Libertines and others like them who separate themselves from the true church of Christ in which one teaches purely his Word and the sacraments are administered according to his commandments."[4]

They add in closing, "For the conclusion we believe that by faith alone we are saved by the mercy of God for the love of his Son Jesus Christ our Lord without our own merits."[5] And then the sixty-seven confessing Walloons sign their confession. Forty-eight men, eighteen women, and one infant—sixty-seven confessing Walloons go by.

24

LOST LETTER
TO THE CORINTHIANS

A book on Calvin, *John Calvin and the Printed Book* by Jean-François Gilmont, tells a rather intriguing story. But first, we need some background. Calvin was kicked out of Geneva in 1538 and went to Strasbourg. While there, he published his first commentary, on the epistle to the Romans. It rolled off the press in 1540. The next year, 1541, the city of Geneva begged Calvin to come back. He wrote to a friend, "There is no place under heaven of which I can have a greater dread."[1] But he felt called by God, and so he went.

When he published his Romans commentary, he was determined to keep going through Paul's epistles. But a roadblock got in the way, a roadblock named Geneva. The church needed Calvin's full attention, and he gave it to them. So, these early years of the 1540s were much consumed by church work. The commentary writing went to the back burner. Calvin eventually managed to find some equilibrium and started writing again. His commentary on 1 Corinthians came out in 1546. And now we get to our story.

After he sent off his commentary on 1 Corinthians to the printer in Strasbourg, Calvin set to work on 2 Corinthians. He finished it in a flurry. From what we can tell, Calvin's record was 17,000 words in about three days. That's one hundred pages. So, at that pace, he finished 2 Corinthians.

In late July 1546, he sent the manuscript—the only copy of the manuscript—by way of a courier to Strasbourg. It was handwritten. No backup. It was typical for a copy to be made, but Calvin did not want to waste the extra time to making a copy. That was likely a miscalculation. Not long after the only copy left with the courier, it went missing. For a whole month, it disappeared. Another roadblock. Back in Geneva was a very anxious Calvin. He wrote, "If I find that my commentary is lost, I have decided to never touch Paul again."[2] His friends weren't of much help. Rather than console him, William Farel wrote to him, "Given that mothers do not neglect their children, you too, should have sent out this fruit of the Lord with greater care."[3] Ouch. Apparently, Farel was reading the account of Job's friends and mistakenly thought it was a command.

But, on September 15, 1546, the word reached Calvin that the manuscript was found safely at Strasbourg and being set to print. No explanations have come down through history, so we're not sure where the manuscript was during this long time it was lost. It might have had something to do with the Schmalkaldic Wars—wars between the Holy Roman Empire, or what was left of it, and the league of German and Swiss princes known as the Schmalkaldic League. We don't know. What we do know is that it caused Calvin a month-load of grief.

This story is interesting because it shows us a Calvin we can relate to. One who frets and worries. One who says desperate things—"I'll never touch Paul again." One who gets anxious. I don't know what image you have of Calvin; I hope it's not the wrongheaded caricature of a dour and mean prophet of gloom. I suspect we tend to think of him as living a somewhat ivory tower life, immune from the challenges we all face in life. Immune from disappointments and roadblocks, frustrations and anxieties. He was not. Maybe we think of him as a super-Christian, always living out the commands of Christ. No, he wasn't that, either. Yet, it is precisely in his humanity that we not only need to see him, but we see him as an example for us. I like stories like this because I lose everything. Keys. I misplace my wallet at least three times a week. I don't like gift cards because, well, I lose them. And I get anxious. We are commanded to be anxious for nothing. But in our frailty, we do. Calvin is part of our company.

If Calvin is known for anything, it's reminding the church of a bedrock faith that God is sovereign over His universe. God is even sovereign over so-called lost manuscripts. We fret and worry and get anxious. We even say desperate things. All the while, we need to rest in God. To trust Him through the roadblocks. As Paul says in the opening lines of 2 Corinthians, "Blessed be the God and Father of our Lord Jesus Christ, the Father of mercies and God of all comfort" (1:3).

25

RIO 1558

The Summer Olympics were held in Rio de Janeiro in 2016. And, as is the nature of such an event, the eyes of the world were upon Rio. But I want to take us back to Rio in 1558. There is a slight backstory here, so let's pick it up. In 1555, a French colony was established in what is now Rio de Janeiro. Then it was simply known as the Guanabara Bay. That original French colony had a number of Huguenots and other Frenchmen committed to the Reformation. The colony was originally open to them, but then it became entrenched in Roman Catholicism and expelled the Huguenots.

Fifteen of those expelled Huguenots boarded a ship to return to France. Shortly after the ship pushed off the Brazilian coast, five of the fifteen took a small boat, lowered it over the ship's edge, and rowed their way back to the shores of Brazil. They were intent on being missionaries. Now, these were not clergy. They were skilled craftsmen and laymen. They were not trained. They had sat in churches and had received solid teaching from the Reformers and especially from John Calvin's students. Eventually, four of them were arrested by the leaders of the colony in Guanabara. They were put into prison and were required to write out a confession of their faith. This was not simply a confession of faith—it would serve to be their death warrant. This was one of the first confessions of faith written during the Reformation, and it is the first confession of faith written in the Americas. It was written a full 218 years before the signing of the Declaration of Independence.

The four men who wrote this confession of faith have largely been lost to us, but we need to remember them. They were Jean du Bourdel, Matthieu Verneuil, Pierre Bourdon, and André la Fon. They prefaced it with this statement: "According to the doctrine of St. Peter, the apostle, in his first epistle, all Christians must always be ready to give a reason for the hope that is in them (1 Peter 3:15), and to do this in all gentleness and kindness."[1] And that is exactly what they proceeded to do. They gave a reason for their hope.

They write in article 11 of their confession: "We believe that forgiveness of sins belongs only to the word of God, of which, as St. Ambrose says, man is only a minister. If man condemns or absolves, it is not of him, but the word of God which is declared."[2] At another point they say:

We believe that Jesus Christ is our only Mediator, Intercessor, and Advocate, through whom we have access to the Father and that, standing justified in His blood, we will be delivered from death. And by whom, standing reconciled, we will obtain full victory over death. As for the saints who have departed we say that they desire our salvation in the fulfillment of the kingdom of God and that the number of the elect be completed. However, we do not need to address ourselves to them, through intercession, in order to obtain certain things because this would be contravening the commandment of God. We who are alive, who are united as members of one body, we ought to pray one for the other as we are taught in many passages of the Holy Scripture.[3]

Then they end their confession of faith with this statement: "This is the answer we give to the articles you sent to us, according to the measure and portion of faith that God has given to us, to whom we pray that it may please Him that our faith not die until it produce fruits worthy of His children."[4] All four men signed their names to this confession, and all four were immediately martyred.

This is the story of the Guanabara Confession of Faith.

26

FORT CAROLINE

Here's a bit of a trick question for you: Where was the first Thanksgiving on American soil? You might be tempted to think of New England. After all, Thanksgiving traditions all point us back to New England. But that guess would be wrong. The first Thanksgiving service, or Thanksgiving day, likely occurred on June 30, 1564, at Fort Caroline, which is near the modern-day city of Jacksonville, Florida.

Fort Caroline was established along the St. Johns River in Florida in 1564 by a group of French Huguenots. In 1562, their leader had made an exploratory trip to Florida and had found this delightful place at the St. Johns River, a place for a settlement. In 1564, two hundred French Huguenot settlers landed in Florida and set up Fort Caroline. They landed in June, and by June 30, they decided to have a service of thanksgiving and celebration of coming to this new world. On this momentous day, the leader of the settlement declared: "On the morrow, about the break of day, I commanded a trumpet to be sounded that, being assembled, we might give God thanks for our favorable and happy arrival. Then we sang a psalm of thanksgiving unto God, beseeching Him, that it would please Him of His Grace, to continue His accustomed goodness toward us, His poor servants, and aid us in all our enterprises that all might turn to His glory and the advancement of our King."[1]

Now, there is a fascinating line in there that should catch our attention. Not only was this the first Thanksgiving, but this was also the first Protestant hymn sing in the New World. Notice that they say they sang a psalm of thanksgiving. When these French Huguenots came, they brought with them the Genevan Psalter. This was the psalter that was produced by John Calvin in Geneva, and it was a significant part of the Huguenots' worship services.

The Spanish also had an interest in Florida. In fact, the Spanish who were sent to settle Florida had a direct order to rid the colony of these French Huguenots. More of the French came in 1565. In fact, another six hundred arrived that summer. These waves of French settlers gave great alarm to the Spanish settlers. The Spanish wanted to control the southern coast of this new world. In September the Spanish, who had settled a little south of Fort Caroline at St. Augustine, attacked and captured Fort Caroline. The Spanish nearly wiped out the Huguenots. The ones who survived the war and survived the massacre made their way back to France. That was the end of the French attempts to colonize Florida.

While they were here, the French taught the American Indians how to sing their songs. These were the Timucuan Indians. They learned to sing the Psalter. In fact, when Timucuan Indians, right around the time of this massacre and before all the

French left, came into contact with European colonists, they would hum a line from the Psalter. If colonists were able to give the line back, the Timucuans knew they were French. But if the colonists had no idea what they were singing, the Timucuans knew that they were Spanish and knew to avoid them.

So, there we have, at sweet Fort Caroline, the first Thanksgiving and the first Protestant hymn sing in America.

27

SHAKESPEARE'S BIBLE

You might be surprised to see a chapter on the Bard in a book on church history, but he nevertheless belongs. William Shakespeare is, of course, known as one of the greatest names in English literature. And one of the fascinating things about Shakespeare is how extensively he quotes and refers to the Bible. In fact, one scholar has put together a book of biblical references in Shakespeare's plays. He compiled a hefty volume, totaling more than eight hundred pages. The Bible is all through Shakespeare.

When we're looking at Shakespeare's use of the Bible, one of the first questions to ask is which version he used. Scholars, after looking at the references in his poems and plays, have concluded that he used three versions. The main version he used is the Geneva Bible, which was published by English and Scottish refugees in Calvin's Geneva in 1560. It's very likely that Shakespeare owned a copy. Shakespeare also refers to the Great Bible, which was commissioned in 1538 by Thomas Cromwell. It first appeared in 1539 and was widely circulated during

Shakespeare's time. The third version was called the Bishop's Bible. A revision of the Great Bible, it was produced by a group of bishops between 1561 and 1564, hence its name.

So, those three Bibles in the English Bible tradition are the versions that Shakespeare used, with the Geneva Bible being the one he went to most often. Scholars have determined this by comparing the text of Shakespeare with the language of the various versions of the time. So for example, in *Richard II*, Shakespeare writes, "Lions make leopards tame. Yea, but not change his spots."[1] That is a reference to Jeremiah 13:23: "Can a leopard change his spots?" Fascinatingly, only the Geneva Bible has "leopard" in that passage. All of the other English versions of Shakespeare's day have the word "cat," as in big cat. But the Geneva Bible has "leopard." So that is the version that Shakespeare was depending on in this case.[2]

After we settle which version of the Bible Shakespeare used, we next turn to see which of the books of the Bible fascinated Shakespeare the most. He seems to be rather taken with the book of Revelation. Again, in *Richard II*, Shakespeare writes, "My name be blotted from the book of life."[3] And that is taken right from Revelation 3:5: "blot out his name out of the book of life." In fact, that shows us that Shakespeare was reading the Bishop's Bible, because it was only the Bishop's Bible that uses the phrase "blot out." The others use the expression "put out."[4]

Of the books of the Bible, Shakespeare quoted the Psalms most often. In *As You Like It*, he writes, "How brief the life of man, the stretching of a span,"[5] referencing Psalm 39:5: "Thou hast made my days as an handbreadth." And in *Timon of Athens*, Shakespeare writes, "Who like a boar too savage does root up his country's peace."[6] This is a reference to Psalm 80:13: "The wild boar out of the wood doth waste it." When the pope called Martin Luther a wild boar, he was also thinking of this text.

These examples only scratch the surface of Shakespeare's use of the Bible in his plays. Sometimes Shakespeare quoted the Bible directly and sometimes he quoted it indirectly. Sometimes what Shakespeare wrote merely resembles and reflects the words of Scripture. But one thing is clear: among the many fascinating things in Shakespeare's plays, you will also find many references to the Bible.

28

1638 IN SCOTLAND

B efore we look at the year 1638 in Scotland, we need to back up just one year and look at the year 1637, and to the specific date of July 23, 1637. We can even go to a specific place, to St. Giles' Cathedral. Now this was not just any cathedral. This cathedral has a great and rich history in the Scottish church. This was the church of John Knox, where he regularly preached. Some more background for this story is in order.

After Elizabeth's death in 1603, James came to the throne. Now James was king of Scotland. In fact, before he was James I of England, he was James VI of Scotland. And he ruled until 1625, and then along came Charles I. Well, James I did not like the Puritans, so he started a program of trying to rout them from the land. In fact, his famous saying is, "I shall make them conform, or I shall harry them out of the land."[1] So, James didn't think very highly of the Puritans, and when Charles I came to the throne, things went from bad to worse for the Puritans.

Charles I had a theological and ecclesiastical henchman, William Laud. Charles I kept promoting Laud up the ranks, and eventually Laud became archbishop of Canterbury. Laud constructed a new version of the Book of Common Prayer and introduced a liturgy that was very much like the old Roman Mass. And then, under the auspices and guidance of Charles I, this Book of Common Prayer was introduced into the Scottish churches. On Sunday, July 23, 1637, this new Book of Common Prayer was read from the pulpit at St. Giles' Church.

There was a particular member of this church who gives us one of the best stories in all of church history. Her name was Jenny Geddes. She was a laywoman in the church. She ran a market stall in town and was a faithful member of St. Giles'. In those days, they didn't have pews in some of these cathedrals and parishioners would bring along stools. They would stand for parts of the service, but then during the sermon they would sit down on their stool.

It came to a part of the sermon, while they were sitting on their stools, that Jenny Geddes heard that the new Book of Common Prayer was going to be read. When she heard what they were reading, she recognized that this was a departure. She then did something that you don't see every day in church. She stood up, grabbed her stool, and hurled it. It fact, as the historical reports have it, she "chucked" it. She chucked it right at the minister's head as he was reading from the Book of Common Prayer.

And while this stool is hurling through the air towards the minister, Jenny Geddes is said to have called out: "The devil cause you colic in the stomach, false thief! Dare you speak the Mass in my ear?"[2] There is a sculpture of the stool that she would have sat on there in St. Giles' as a memorial to her. That was in 1637.

In the next year, 1638, the Scots formed the National Covenant. These are the folks we know as the Covenanters. In 1640, the Scottish Parliament endorsed and adopted the National Covenant. In the next couple years and then through the whole next decade, the English Civil War broke out. It all started with Jenny Geddes not wanting to sit under some Roman-style Mass and chucking her stool at the minister's head.

29

THE PURSUIT OF HAPPINESS: ACCORDING TO WILLIAM AMES

One of the most beloved Puritan books is a systematic theology by William Ames. Ames was born in November of 1576, and he died in November of 1633. Ames was a Cambridge man. He was at Christ's College, and while he was there he came under the influence of William Perkins. Ames got caught up in some politics in Cambridge, and he was a bit too vocal. He found himself on the outs with the vice-chancellor of the university. And so, he was politely asked to leave. Bishops around England blocked his appointment to various parishes, and so he, like so many of the Puritans during this time, went to Holland. He was there for the controversy of Jacobus Arminius, and was there in Holland at the Synod of Dort in the 1610s.

Ames wrote many books, but we're going to consider just one, his systematic theology. For Ames, and for the Puritans in general, theology was not the dry-bones stuff for academics.

We get a clue to how he thinks about theology by his title. He called his book *The Marrow of Theology*. The Latin is *Medulla Theologiae*. Theology is not dry bones; far from it. Theology is the life-giving substance in the bone. Theology is marrow. So we have to appreciate his title.

We also get a clue about how he thinks about theology from the opening two pages of his book, even from his very first line. Ames says, "Theology is the doctrine, or teaching, of living to God."[1] He goes on to say that theology is an art like the other arts studied in the university. It is an academic discipline. Our knowledge of theology can be advanced by the application of our minds to the task, by industry. Ames is quick to point out, however, that theology is unlike all the other disciplines. It has an entirely different source, an entirely different outcome. And both the source and the outcome are the same. The source is God and His revelation, and the outcome is God in His glory, and our enjoyment of Him.

Theology is not just *thinking* toward God; theology is *living* toward God. Now up until this point, Ames is closely following Thomas Aquinas and his definition of theology. Thomas, the medieval theologian, says theology is taught by God, teaches about God, and leads to God. Thomas will later expand on this idea of theology leading to God by telling us that theology leads us to *worship* God. The end of theology is worship. Theology is doxology.

Once Ames defines what theology is, with a little help from his friend Thomas Aquinas, Ames reaches all the way back to the days of the Greek philosophers. He reaches back to Plato and Aristotle and the age-old discussion of what constitutes the good life. What is happiness, and what brings happiness? To get at this, Ames uses two Greek words. The first is *euzoia*, and the second is *eudaimonia*. Now, *euzoia* means living well. We would simply say, the good life. And *eudaimonia* means living happily. We would simply say, happiness. And then Ames said theology is this. Theology is the good life and theology is happiness.

You want the good life? You want happiness? Be a theologian. As Ames closes off these first two pages he writes: "Theology therefore, is to us, the ultimate and the noblest of all the exact teaching arts. It is a guide and master plan for our highest end, sent in a special manner from God, treating of divine things, tending towards God, and leading man to God."[2] Theology is living the Godward life, the happy life.

THE MODERN AGE

■

30

ROBINSON CRUSOE'S CONVERSION

Shipwrecked, a castaway, menaced by cannibals and pirates. This is the story of *Robinson Crusoe*, the consummate adventure story. The book was written by Daniel Defoe and published in 1719.

First, a little bit about Daniel Defoe. He's buried in Bunhill Fields, which is a cemetery in London for Puritans. It is the Nonconformist cemetery. Actually, the portion where Defoe was buried was bombed out during World War II, and the graves in that area had to be moved. An obelisk commemorates the spot where Defoe's grave had been.

In 1719, he published his book, and we know it as *Robinson Crusoe*. The full title, though, is a bit more informative:

The Life and Strange Surprizing Adventures of Robinson Crusoe, Of York, Mariner: Who lived Eight and Twenty Years, all alone in an un-inhabited Island on the Coast of

*America, near the Mouth of the Great River of Oroono-
que; Having been cast on Shore by Shipwreck, wherein all
the Men perished but himself. With An Account how he
was at last as strangely deliver'd by Pyrates.*

And that's just the title page.

As the book begins the tale, Robinson Crusoe sets sail from
Hull, England, in 1651. He is eventually shipwrecked and washes
ashore on an island. He will spend twenty-eight years on his
island. Crusoe offers a textured account, with meticulous detail,
so much so that many readers found the level of detail in the story
incredible. They were convinced that it was a true story and that
Defoe had simply found a diary and recounted its narrative.

A fascinating part of the tale is the account of Crusoe's conversion. Early in his time on the island, we begin to see some
glimpses of his awareness of God. He came from a religious
family, but he turned his back on all of that when he set out
to become a sailor. But he makes references to providence and
other generic references to God. After a few years on the island,
things appear to be going well but are not truly going well for
him. At one point, he simply stops and cries out to God with
a very simple prayer: "Lord, have mercy."[1] Then he remembers
that he has a Bible with him.

Robinson Crusoe starts reading his Bible. As he does so,
he decides that he will read from the New Testament. At one
point, Crusoe writes in his diary:

In the morning I took the Bible; and beginning at
the New Testament, I began seriously to read it, and

imposed upon myself to read a while every morning and every night; not tying myself to the number of chapters, but long as my thoughts should engage me. It was not long after I set seriously to this work till I found my heart more deeply and sincerely affected with the wickedness of my past life. The impression of my dream revived; and the words, "All these things have not brought thee to repentance," ran seriously through my thoughts. I was earnestly begging of God to give me repentance, when it happened providentially, the very day, that, reading the Scripture, I came to these words: "He is exalted a Prince and a Savior, to give repentance and to give remission." I threw down the book; and with my heart as well as my hands lifted up to heaven, in a kind of ecstasy of joy, I cried out aloud, "Jesus, thou son of David! Jesus, thou exalted Prince and Savior! Give me repentance!"[2]

You can read the rest of the story for yourself. Robinson Crusoe had many more years on his island before (spoiler alert) he was rescued. But through it all, he continued reading his Bible and trusting in the Savior he met on the island, the Lord Jesus Christ.

31

JONATHAN EDWARDS' FAVORITE WORD

Jonathan Edwards was a prominent pastor and theologian during the First Great Awakening of the eighteenth century. He is best known for his sermon "Sinners in the Hands of an Angry God," which is famous for its vivid imagery of hell and judgment. For this reason, he has acquired a reputation among those who have only a passing familiarity with him as being rather angry himself, full of venom and spite—the quintessential fire-and-brimstone preacher.

Some likely think that this is all Edwards ever talked about. Some think his favorite word was *judgment* or maybe *anger*. It might surprise those who hold to such a view to know what Edwards' favorite word actually was. This word, and its synonyms, are sprinkled generously throughout his writings. The word is *happy*.

Happiness, joy, sweetness, delight, even relish—Edwards explored how we can attain them. How are we made happy?

The question is of utmost significance, because not only does it help us understand Edwards but it also helps us get at that nagging, ultimate question: Why am I here?

Edwards grew up on the Westminster Shorter Catechism. He learned from the first question that the chief end of man is "to glorify God and enjoy Him forever." Our culture tells us that true happiness and true joy come from serving the self. But this is a false idea. Jesus exposed this idea as a lie: "For whoever would save his life will lose it, but whoever loses his life for my sake will find it" (Matt. 16:25). We were made for God, made with a singular purpose: to glorify Him. And as we glorify Him and as we live for and live toward Him, we find our soul's true joy. This is how we are made happy. In fact, Edwards even liked to use the word *happified*. We are happified when we glorify God and enjoy Him.

Finding true joy in God is a central theme in Edwards' writing: "The doctrine of God's sovereignty has very often appeared an exceeding pleasant, bright, and sweet doctrine to me; and absolute sovereignty is what I love to ascribe to God."[1]

There's also the word *sweet*. At one point in the *Institutes*, John Calvin speaks of a saving knowledge of God as a *sensus sauvitatis*, a sense of sweetness.

Elsewhere, Edwards says:

God himself is the great good which [the redeemed] are brought to the possession and enjoyment of by redemption. He is the highest good and the sum of all that good which Christ purchased. God is the inheritance of the saints; he is the portion of their souls. God is their wealth and treasure, their food, their life, their dwelling place, their ornament and diadem, and their everlasting honor and glory.[2]

By talking about joy and sweetness and relishing and enjoying God, Edwards was in good company. So David tells us in Psalm 34:8: "Oh, taste and see that the LORD is good! Blessed is the man who takes refuge in him!" In Psalm 63, David writes: "O God, you are my God; earnestly I seek you; my soul thirsts for you; my flesh faints for you, as in a dry and weary land where there is no water. So I have looked upon you in the sanctuary, beholding your power and glory. Because your steadfast love is better than life, my lips will praise you" (vv. 1–3). A few verses later, he adds, "In the shadow of your wings I will sing for joy" (v. 7).

Edwards knew about sin. He knew of God's wrath against sin. He did not shrink away from speaking of judgment. He preached about these words often, no doubt. But comb through his sermons and books and you'll see he gives far greater room to the good news of our happiness and joy in God. So, be happified. Serve and love and enjoy—and even relish—God.

32

DAVID BRAINERD'S
HEBREW DICTIONARY

Historians tend to visit strange places. They like to visit cemeteries. They track down obscure, out-of-the-way historical markers. They also like to visit libraries, especially libraries with rare collections and rare finds. One such library is the main library of Princeton University. This library holds over seven million books and has nearly fifty thousand linear feet of manuscripts. It's enough to make a historian giddy.

Among the many interesting millions of books housed in the Firestone Library is one book in particular worth spending some time on. To get a sense of this book, it measures about four inches wide, about six inches in length, and about four inches thick. It has a unique and rather fascinating binding. It is actually bound in otter skin. Yes, otter skin. And not only is it bound in otter skin, but it's painted with blue and red stripes; and it's painted in a style that's the characteristic painting of the

Eastern Woodland Indians. So we have an otter-skin-bound, painted Hebrew dictionary.

It is a dictionary of Hebrew and also of Aramaic. It was first published in Basel in 1654, and somehow it made its way into the hands of David Brainerd. When David Brainerd died, it passed on to Jonathan Edwards. So it was actually in possession of Jonathan Edwards. In January of 1758, Jonathan Edwards began his tenure as president of Princeton University. His tenure was rather short. He died on March 22, 1758. Many books from his personal library passed to the university. Many others were passed on to family members. The Hebrew dictionary went to the family. Eventually some family member gave it to Princeton University.

This is an intriguing book for a number of reasons. First, there's the otter skin cover with painted stripes. If you ever would use the word *cool* to describe the binding of a Hebrew dictionary, this is the time. It was either bound by Brainerd and painted by him with techniques he learned from the Indians he was a missionary to, or it was bound and painted by the Indians he served.

Second, this is a Hebrew dictionary. This should encourage all Hebrew teachers out there that their labors are not in vain. As an itinerant missionary to Indians in the colonies of New Jersey and Pennsylvania, David Brainerd would have traveled light. But he had a Hebrew dictionary.

And third, this is an intriguing book because it belonged to David Brainerd.

David Brainerd was a missionary to the American Indians in the 1700s. He started first in the colony of New York among the Mohicans for a brief time. Then he went down to the colonies of New Jersey and Pennsylvania. There, he took the gospel to the Delaware Indians as a missionary. He even went deep into the woods of central Pennsylvania and was a missionary to the Susquehanna Indians.

Brainerd started off his life as a farmer. When he was eighteen years old, he inherited a farm, and he farmed it for about three years. And then, when he was twenty-one, he had a conversion. At his conversion, he says, he was given a "hearty desire to exalt [God] and to 'seek first His Kingdom.'"[1] About two months after his conversion, he went to Yale. He entered Yale right at the time of the Great Awakening, 1740–1742. And in 1742, Brainerd was very much a proponent of this time of awakening. He was concerned for the state of the souls of some of his professors. In fact, at one point, David Brainerd, a student at Yale, said directly to one of his Yale professors that he had "no more grace than this chair."[2] For that, David Brainerd found himself expelled. A year later, he began his work among the American Indians.

By 1746, after just a few short years of missionary work, Brainerd was so ill that he simply could not continue. We know now that he had tuberculosis. In fact, he had tuberculosis from the time of his first year at Yale. When he became seriously ill, he left Pennsylvania and headed north. He made his way to the town of Northampton in the colony of Massachusetts and specifically to the home of Jonathan Edwards. While he was there, Brainerd shared his diary with Jonathan Edwards. Edwards used it to write *The Life of David Brainerd*. In Edwards' lifetime this was his most popular book. Brainerd died in 1747 at the age of twenty-nine in the home of Jonathan Edwards.

Brainerd's epitaph, which most likely was written by Edwards, simply reads, "A faithful and laborious missionary to the Stockbridge, Delaware, and Susquehannah Indians." Not only was he a faithful missionary, he was also a faithful student. And so he had in his possession his Hebrew dictionary bound in otter skin and painted with red and blue stripes.

33

SLAVE, MINUTEMAN, PASTOR

Do you know Lemuel Haynes? If not, you should. Lemuel Haynes was born on July 18, 1753. He was born in Connecticut, but as a five-month-old he found himself in Massachusetts. He was an indentured servant, or slave. He was also educated, and he was educated in a strong Calvinist family and in a strong Calvinist Congregational church. In 1773, at twenty years old, Lemuel Haynes was converted and professed his faith in Jesus Christ. The next year, 1774, he was again set free, and this time from his bondage as a slave. Haynes was a free man.

These events coincided with the fomenting of the revolutionary spirit and the soon eruption of the American Revolutionary War. Haynes enlisted as a minuteman, and he served as a soldier in the Continental Army. He fought right from the beginning of the war as America declared independence from Britain, and he fought through the early campaigns. Following the war, Haynes took up a pastorate, and he also took to writing. For thirty years, he pastored in Rutland, Vermont.

He was the first African American to pastor a predominantly white congregation. He then spent the last eleven years of his life pastoring in West Granville, New York. Haynes died on September 28, 1833.

As mentioned, Lemuel Haynes also wrote a number of items. In fact, a beautiful piece that he wrote was called "The Character of a Spiritual Watchman." Using the designation of "Spiritual Watchman" is Haynes' way of referring to a pastor. He starts by emphasizing that a pastor must have natural gifts and a good education. It is a given that he would have these natural gifts, that he would be educated in the Word and the languages, and that he would be educated in theology. Haynes then discusses the pastor's character traits. He lists five character traits in all.

Haynes starts off by pointing out that the shepherd must love the flock. The second character trait is wisdom and prudence. The third is patience. The fourth is courage and fortitude. And the fifth is vigilance. While Haynes aimed these five characteristics at pastors, all Christians need each one of these. Whether we are in the pulpit or in the pew, we all need to be marked by these character traits. Now as we think about these for the pastoral ministry, I think in reality we all need these as Christians. We all need to be marked by these character traits.

Consider the fourth character trait, that of courage and fortitude. This is always necessary. Challenges and challengers abound. It's easy to lose heart, to compromise convictions, to cower. Haynes helps us see how important courage and fortitude are. He writes: "Courage and fortitude must constitute a part of the character of a gospel minister. A sentinel who is worthy of that station will not fear the formidable appearance of the enemy, nor tremble at their menaces. None of these things will move him; neither will he count his life dear unto him to defend a cause so very important. He has the spirit of intrepid Nehemiah."[1] Haynes' reference to Nehemiah is specifically Nehemiah 6:11: "Should such a man as I run away?" The spiritual watchman, as Haynes points out, stands fast in the faith.

In his own day, Lemuel Haynes took a stand. He took a stand for the gospel. In his area in Vermont he was surrounded by Unitarian Universalists, and yet he took a stand for the faithful and bold proclamation of the gospel. And of course, in his day he was surrounded by slavery. And he took a stand against that. Lemuel Haynes knew a thing or two about courage and fortitude.

Looking at our own context today, we see that we are called to speak the gospel to a culture that is not always that receptive and welcoming of it. We are called to stand for convictions in a culture that is growing increasingly hostile to those convictions. May we have this courage and fortitude of which Lemuel Haynes, the former slave, the minuteman, and the pastor, spoke.

34

BEN CHIMES IN ON GEORGE

You might be thinking this is Big Ben, London's iconic clock tower. But it's not. It's America's own Ben, Benjamin Franklin. And the George in question is George Whitefield, the great evangelist of the Great Awakening. You could easily refer to these two as the odd couple. One a sinner, one a saint. But something connected these two men. Or, rather, something drew Franklin to Whitefield. Of course, George Whitefield knew of Ben Franklin. Franklin was a celebrity. So was Whitefield. It would make sense that when Whitefield made his first visit to Philadelphia, these two would meet each other. But the connection between the two went deeper than a customary meeting.

In his autobiography, Benjamin Franklin devotes a number of pages to his recollections of his friendship with George Whitefield. He introduces Whitefield in his autobiography with this line: "In 1739, arrived among us from England, the Reverend Mr. Whitefield, who had made himself remarkable there as an itinerant preacher. He was at first permitted to preach in some of our churches, but the clergy taking a dislike to him soon refused him their pulpits, and he was obliged to preach in the fields."[1]

Well, that was nothing new for Whitefield. He was used to being uninvited from pulpits back in old England. One of his sermons he liked to preach was titled "The Almost Christian." Whitefield would say something to this effect: You know who the almost Christian is? It's the one who is resting in simply being a churchgoer. Almost Christians are those who rest in their baptism as infants in the Anglican Church. But they are not true Christians. They are almost Christians. So it probably shouldn't surprise us that after a few of those kinds of sermons in Anglican churches, Whitefield found himself uninvited from pulpits. That did not stop Whitefield. He simply turned to the open fields. Or, as in the case of Philadelphia, he went to the open streets.

In his autobiography, Franklin goes on to say of Whitefield, "I observe the extraordinary influence of his oratory on his hearers, and how much they admired and respected him, not withstanding his common abuse of them by assuring them they were naturally half beasts and half devils."[2] Of course, what Franklin is referring to here is Whitefield's Calvinism. And as a Calvinist, he understood that people were sinners and they needed to be saved. The question is, What do we need to be saved from? Because we are sinners, we need to be saved from the judgment to come and the outpouring of God's wrath. To call us half-beasts is actually an insult to beasts. We are worse. We have contempt for God.

Franklin was anything but a Calvinist. In fact, at one point,

Franklin said, "My mother grieves because one of her sons is an Arian, another an Arminian."[3] Well, actually, Ben Franklin was both an Arian and an Arminian, and so he wasn't too keen on Whitefield's Calvinism. But they developed a friendship nevertheless. In fact, at one point, Whitefield had founded an orphanage in Georgia, and he would take up collections at his revival meetings for these orphans. The naysayers and the critics claimed that Whitefield was only lining his own pockets. Franklin spoke directly to that and defended him. He wrote of Whitefield's character: "So these enemies of Whitefield's, they said he was going to apply these collections to his own private profit. But I who was intimately acquainted with him, being employed in the printing of his sermons and the printing of his journals, etc., never had the least suspicion of his integrity, but am to this day decidedly of opinion that he was in all his conduct, a perfectly honest man."[4]

Franklin was not simply impressed by Whitefield's oratory—that he was a great speaker to crowds. What he was impressed by in addition to that was that what was in front of him was a man of integrity. Now, he was a great speaker, there's no doubt. In fact, Franklin has a great story he tells in this regard:

I happened soon after to attend one of his sermons in the course of which I perceived he intended to finish with the collection. And I silently resolved, "He should get nothing from me." I had in my pocket a handful of copper money, 3 or 4 silver dollars, and 5 Spanish gold coins. As he proceeded I began to soften, and concluded to give the coppers. Another stroke of his oratory made me ashamed of that and determined me to give the silver. And he finished so admirably that I emptied my pocket wholly into the collector's dish. Coppers, silver, gold, and all.[5]

That is Ben chiming in on George.

35

FRANCIS GRIMKÉ

Francis Grimké was born in 1850 as a slave on a plantation near Charleston, South Carolina. He had a white father who died when he was rather young. And, according to the law at that time, he became the property of his white half-brother. Initially, his half-brother treated him well. Grimké and his other siblings, along with his mother, lived in town basically as free persons. But then something happened that caused a terrible change in his half-brother. As Grimké was moving into his upper teens, his half-brother brought him into his home as a house slave and, by all accounts, treated him very harshly. During the Civil War, one of Grimké's other brothers managed to run away successfully. So Francis himself attempted to run away during the Civil War. He was caught and returned, but after the war he was finally emancipated.

Grimké went with one of his brothers to study at Lincoln University in Pennsylvania, receiving his bachelor's degree in 1870. He then ventured on to New Jersey and became a student at Princeton Theological Seminary. He studied in earnest from 1875 to 1878. He was in the class of the last group of students at Princeton to have Charles Hodge as his theology professor for all three years. Upon his graduation, Grimké was ordained as a minister in the Presbyterian Church.

In 1928, on his fiftieth anniversary of being in ministry, Grimké wrote of his appreciation for Princeton in reference to early twentieth-century liberal Christianity: "The findings of higher critics, the rationalist tendencies within the church . . . ; the dogmatic and arrogant assumptions and declarations of science, that would banish God from the universe or limit his power, all of that has not affected me in the least, nor affected my perfect faith in the Bible."[1] That's a testament to the education that he received at Princeton Seminary under professors such as Charles Hodge.

After graduating, he served as pastor of Fifteenth Street Presbyterian Church in Washington, D.C., from 1878 to 1885. In 1885, he began serving as a pastor in a Presbyterian church in Jacksonville, Florida, but he missed Washington, D.C., and the Fifteenth Street Presbyterian Church and returned in 1889. He would serve there until 1928, when he retired. He died in 1937.

As a student of Princeton Theological Seminary, Grimké had read John Calvin, and he admired him throughout his ministry. At one point, after reading an address on John Calvin, he wrote in his diary:

> As I laid it aside, more profoundly impressed than ever before by the character and work of John Calvin there went up from my heart the earnest prayer that when my

life ends here that I too may be remembered because of some things I have said or done in bringing men face to face with life and its great and solemn responsibilities for which they must answer at the bar of God. To feel, as John Calvin felt, the sovereignty of God and to get others to feel the same, . . . is a great achievement and will go on working for good long after we are gone.[2]

That was Grimké's mission, to get others to feel the sovereignty of God.

36

B.B. AND ANNIE

B.B. and Annie. This is the story of a marriage between Benjamin Breckinridge Warfield and Annie Pierce Kinkead. We know Warfield as the great stalwart of Princeton Theological Seminary—he is sometimes called the Lion of Princeton. He was a significant figure in the Fundamentalist-Modernist Controversy. He was a mentor to J. Gresham Machen and laid the groundwork for the work of Machen and others who fought the good fight within the Presbyterian Church and in other denominations in the twentieth century.

But I want to talk about Warfield's marriage. Warfield was born in 1851 in Lexington, Kentucky. A year later, Annie Pierce Kinkead was born, also in Lexington. The Warfields were members of Second Presbyterian Church in Lexington while the Kinkeads were members of First Presbyterian Church. But even though Benjamin and Annie went to different churches, they apparently spent a lot of time together. Annie's family was a family of lawyers and a family that had generals in the Revolutionary War. They were a well-established family and a well-heeled family. Her father even successfully defended Abraham Lincoln at one point. Warfield's family was also well heeled. They were also a family of lawyers and had large cattle farms. In fact, Warfield's father wrote a book on cattle breeding. That was the career that Warfield was headed toward before he decided to go into the ministry and pursue theological scholarship.

Benjamin and Annie were married on August 3, 1876. Immediately after their wedding, they went to Europe and spent an entire year there while Warfield was studying at the University of Leipzig, Germany. While they were in Europe, they would take long walks in the mountains. On one of these walks, something happened. One of Warfield's colleagues at Princeton, O.T. Allis, recounts the event:

> In his distinguished and eminently successful career there was an element of tragedy. After graduating from the seminary at the age of twenty-five, he had married and he had taken his wife into Germany. A honeymoon in which he studied at Leipzig. On a walking trip in the Harz mountains they were overtaken by a terrific thunderstorm. It was such a shattering experience for Mrs. Warfield she never fully recovered from the shock to her nervous system and was more or less of an invalid during the rest of her life. I used to see them walking together and the gentleness of his manner was striking proof of the loving care with which he surrounded her. They had no children. During the years spent at Princeton he rarely, if ever, was absent for any length of time. Mrs. Warfield required his constant attention and care.[1]

Warfield's former student and younger colleague at Princeton, J. Gresham Machen, adds this:

I have faint recollections of her walking up and down in front of the house in the early years of my Princeton life but even that diversion has long been denied her. I never spoke to her. Her trouble has been partly nervous, and she has seen hardly anyone except Dr. Warfield, but she remained, they say, until the end a very brilliant woman. Dr. Warfield used to read to her during certain definite hours every day. For many, many years he has never been away from her more than two hours at a time. It has been some ten years since he left Princeton. What the effect of her death upon him will be I do not know. I think, however, that he will feel dreadfully lost without her.[2]

Warfield's life, as Machen tells us, was rather circumscribed. He and Annie lived in the Hodge house on campus, the former home of Charles Hodge. It was a large home, which was good for Warfield, because he could fill it with books. Only a few steps from his side door stood Alexander Hall, where Warfield taught his classes. Just past the quad stood Miller Chapel, where Warfield attended chapel during the week and services on the Lord's Day. His world was Princeton Theological Seminary. He taught students. He read, reviewed, and wrote books. And he cared for his tender wife.

Mrs. Armstrong, the wife of a faculty member at Princeton, said after Annie's death in 1915, "He has only two interests in his life—his work, and Mrs. Warfield, and now that she is gone there may be danger of his using himself up rather quickly."[3]

That is the love story, albeit the tragic love story, of B.B. and Annie.

37

MACHEN AND MOUNTAINS

"I do love the mountains, and I have loved them ever since I can remember anything at all."[1] That quote comes to us from J. Gresham Machen. Machen was born in 1881, and he died on January 1, 1937. Machen left behind a great legacy. He left behind the legacy of a denomination, the Orthodox Presbyterian Church. He left behind the legacy of Westminster Theological Seminary. And he also left behind the legacy of a number of great books, like his classic text *Christianity and Liberalism*. That book of Machen's is perhaps even more necessary and more urgent, given the challenges that the church of today is facing, than when Machen first wrote it back in 1923.

Machen wrote many other books and also a lot of other shorter writings. One of them is a piece that was published in *Christianity Today* titled "Mountains and Why We Love Them." Machen did, as he says in this piece, love the mountains.

Machen grew up in Baltimore, but his family would vacation up in Bar Harbor, Maine. His first exposure to the mountains were the rugged mountains of New England. And then when he graduated from Johns Hopkins University, his parents gave him as a graduation present a trip to Switzerland. There, in Switzerland he had his first encounter with the Alps.

Throughout his life, and as time permitted and his duties allowed, he would find himself back in Switzerland, and back on these Alps. And he's speaking in this piece, "Mountains and Why We Love Them," of what he learned. He remembers in particular one time when he was standing on the Matterhorn. He could look out over, essentially, all of Europe. And as he looked out from that vantage point he says, "You think of the great men whose memories you love, the men who have struggled there in those countries below you, who have struggled for light and freedom, struggled for beauty, struggled above all for God's Word."[2]

These are, of course, the lands of Luther, the lands of Calvin, the lands of the great Reformation. And then Machen is seeing what is happening in these lands. He's seeing the crumbling of the Reformers' efforts in the twentieth century. As a mountain lifts you up and gives you a perspective over the horizon, so those who are living in the modern world need a perspective. They need to be lifted up above their limited horizon. Machen says, "When I do that," when he has this kind of mountaintop perspective, "I cannot for the life of me see how any man with even the slightest knowledge of history can help recognizing the fact that we are living in a time of sad decadence. A decadence only thinly disguised by the material achievements of our age, which already are beginning to pall on us like a new toy."[3] Modernity, Machen intones, has proposed life without God. How bleak.

Machen doesn't just want to end on a sour note, however. Certainly, there is a negative thing he has to learn from these experiences of climbing mountains, but there's also something very positive. And so, at the end of this piece Machen says, "There's only one alternative to this modernist worldview," this worldview that futilely attempts to push God out. Machen then simply declares: "The alternative is that there is a God. A God who in His own good time will bring forward great men again to do His will, great men to resist the tyranny of experts, and lead humanity out again into the realms of light and freedom. Great men above all who will be the messengers of His grace. There is far above any earthly mountain peak of vision a God high and lifted up, who although He is infinitely exalted, yet he cares for His children among men."[4]

This is why Machen loved mountains and the God who made them.

38

MACHEN ON 11/11

On April 6, 1917, America joined a war that had been raging in Europe since 1914. It was called the War to End All Wars; we know it as World War I. At the time, Machen was at Princeton. He had been there for quite some time. He was a student at both the university, in a master's program in philosophy, and at the seminary. After a brief time of doctoral studies in Germany, he was appointed an instructor at Princeton Theological Seminary.

Of course, he had been following the events of the war. Ever since war broke out in Europe, Machen was paying close attention, as it looked like America would enter the war. Right after Congress declared war on April 6, Machen wrote in a letter, "I feel as though I ought to have some immediate part in the manifold work that is going forward."[1] He looked into being a chaplain but he realized that, as a chaplain, he would be an officer. He did not think he would have enough connection with the enlisted men as an officer. He looked into being an ambulance driver, but in the end, Machen settled on working for the YMCA.

In those days, the YMCA provided social services for soldiers. They would help them write money orders to get their checks back home. They would give them letters and pens to help them keep up with the folks back home. They would give soldiers magazines and books. And they would also make them hot chocolate. In fact, at one point, Machen wrote, "I have worn one uniform ever since leaving Paris and it is now all spotted up with hot chocolate."[2]

He also witnessed very closely the horrors of war. He wrote of the planes and the shells, how they were relentless overhead. At one point, he called it "the concussion of the air. . . . It is a rather brutal violation of the two elements, earth and air. I hate it, as I hate the whole business of war. But I am convinced that in the interests of peace, the Allies have simply got to win."[3] At one point, Machen said, "The scenes that I have stressed can never be forgotten, but it is not so easy to make any one else realize what they were like."[4]

That peace that Machen wrote about finally did come. On the eleventh hour of the eleventh day of the eleventh month in 1918, the armistice went into effect. It is known as Armistice Day, or, in the United Kingdom, as Remembrance Day. We now know it as Veterans Day in the United States. It is when World War I came to an end. On that day, Machen wrote a letter home, exclaiming: "The Lord's name be praised. Hardly before have I known what true thanksgiving is. Nothing but the exuberance of the Psalms of David, accompanied with the psaltery on an instrument of ten strings could begin to do justice to the joy of this hour. Bless the Lord, O my soul. It seems to me that the hills must break forth into singing, 'Peace at last and praise to God!'"[5]

One of the things that Machen noticed the most after the eleventh hour of the eleventh day of the eleventh month was the silence. He reveled in the silence. He wrote: "But we heard something greater by far in contrast with the familiar roar of war, namely, the silence of the misty morning. I think I can venture upon the paradox, that was a silence that could really be heard." Machen continues, "I suppose it was the most eloquent, the most significant silence in the history of the world."[6]

It would be another four months before Machen was able to leave France and make his way back to Princeton. He helped soldiers as they readjusted from the horrors of war and what they had seen and prepared them to return home to their families and to their work. When Machen returned to Princeton in 1918, he had a renewed purpose, a renewed sense of calling. He would need it, because the next few years would engage him in another battle, this time a theological battle. This time, he would be engaged in a battle for the soul of his own denomination and a battle for the faith.

39

ON AND OFF THE TRACK

Eric Liddell was an early Olympic star, known as "the Flying Scotsman." He is famous for his feats on the track at the 1924 Paris Olympics. But he also lived an interesting life off the track.

Though he was Scottish, Liddell was actually born in China in 1902, and he would die there in 1945. His parents were missionaries and Scottish Presbyterians; his father was a doctor and did medical missionary work. When Liddell was a young man, he was sent back to Scotland for boarding school, and he later attended university in Scotland. At university, he excelled both in his studies (with a focus on the sciences) and in athletics. Rugby and sprinting were his two main sports, and he was quite the force at 100 meters and at 200 meters.

It was clear early on that Liddell was destined for the Olympics, and he set his sights on Paris in 1924. However, a scheduling issue meant that he would not compete in the 100, his best event. The first heat in that distance was set for a Sunday, and Liddell, as a devout Scottish Presbyterian, would not run on the Sabbath.

So, Liddell trained for and competed in the 400 meters as well as the 200 meters. In the 200, he earned a bronze. But to everyone's surprise, in the 400—a middle-distance race, as opposed to the sprint distances in which he specialized—Liddell won gold.

In fact, one of the newspapers said, not only was Liddell's 400-meter win a surprise, it was also quite the spectacle. He had an unusual running style; he would throw his head back and flail his arms as if he were hurling himself down the track. One newspaper said, "He is remembered . . . as probably the ugliest runner who ever won an Olympic championship."[1]

Off the track, his life was also fascinating. The year after the Olympics, he left Scotland and went to China. He could have stayed in Scotland, of course. He was quite a celebrity and could have entered into any career or position he wanted. But he wanted to go back to China and serve as a missionary. He was there for twenty years, until his death in 1945.

He had a variety of roles as a missionary, including as a teacher to first- and second-grade Chinese children. These were children of wealthy Chinese businessmen and government officials. Liddell recognized that these children would very likely go on to have positions of influence themselves, and so he saw it as a great responsibility to try not only to teach them but also to see them come to Christ and to train them up in the gospel. In addition to being a teacher, he was also superintendent of the Sunday school and, of course, he trained his young charges in all varieties of sports and athletics.

During World War II, the Japanese invaded China. They interned the Westerners, including the missionaries. Liddell had plenty of warning, and he did manage to get his family to safety, but he decided to stay behind and was imprisoned. He was, for all intents and purposes, a doctor. He had a doctor for a father, and he studied the sciences at university. He practiced medicine through much of his time as a missionary in China. He thought those skills might be useful to his fellow prisoners in the internment camp, so he decided to stay and to help. But the conditions of the camp were horrible, and the squalor caught Liddell in its grasp. He died in China, the land of his birth, in an internment camp on February 21, 1945.

Before Liddell stepped up to the starting block for the 400-meter final at Paris in 1924, a team masseur gave him a slip of paper, and on it were these words from 1 Samuel 2:30: "Those who honor me I will honor." Eric Liddell sought to live in light of those words on and off the track.

40

READ ANY
GOOD BOOKS LATELY?

In 2 Timothy 4:13, Paul writes: "When you come, bring the cloak that I left with Carpus at Troas, also the books, and above all the parchments." We essentially have the voicing of the needs of a tired, old man. The evenings are growing chillier and he needs his cloak, and for once in his very busy life, he finds himself with time on his hands.

What we are seeing here is what matters most to Paul. As John Calvin says, commenting on this verse, "The apostle had not given over reading though he was already preparing for death."[1] So Paul wants his books, and he especially wants his parchments. Much effort has been expended in trying to identify these books and parchments. Most assume the parchments to be Scripture, as Paul asks for these "above all."

As for the books, that's another story. Were they Plato? Aristotle? *Rhetoric*, perhaps? Or *Logic*? Or *Nicomachean Ethics*? Maybe there was a history, perhaps Paul's well-thumbed-through

Thucydides. Maybe one of the books was Aratus; Paul liked to quote that poet, and he quoted him while he was on Mars Hill in Athens. We forget sometimes that Paul was a scholar.

Whatever the identity of the books and the parchments, we do know something for certain about Paul: he loved to read. Books lay out for us the whole breadth of the human condition, reflect the best of man's creative work as God's image bearer, and point out our need for a Savior, to the glory of God. This concept may be somewhat foreign to us, as reading has fallen on hard times in our technologized culture—entertainment, preferably the visual kind, is in. What Neil Postman said two decades ago is probably all the more true in our day. We have "amused ourselves to death."[2] We have anesthetized ourselves to where we are comfortably numb. *Fahrenheit 451* is, I'm afraid, off the mark. There's really no need to burn books. People aren't reading them anyway.

But what happens when we read? I can tell you a little bit about what's happened to me when I read. I've read G.C. Berkouwer's *The Providence of God* and Jonathan Edwards' *A History of the Work of Redemption*, and since reading those books, I've never thought about God and what He's doing in the world in the same way. I've read Dietrich Bonhoeffer's *The Cost of Discipleship* and his letters from his six-by-nine-foot cell at Tegel prison, and I've been made aware that I have only a faint idea of what it means to be a disciple of Jesus Christ.

I've read Flannery O' Connor, Ernest Hemingway, John Steinbeck, and William Faulkner, and as I've read them I've been entertained and I've even been shocked. I've even been brought to repentance when I've been touched by their unveiling of the rich texture of humanity.

I've allowed the prince of Denmark to remind me how stale and flat and unprofitable all the promises of life under the sun seem. I've read the tale of Lady Macbeth and of how unhealthy ambition can breed in the dark chambers of the human heart and produce the offspring of hatred and evil. I've learned of the emptiness of what so many value and think to be so worthwhile.

I've read John Milton, who laments the great loss of what was ours as Adam and Eve leave the garden. I've listened in as Milton has them waste away the hours in endless bickering, before Milton then takes Adam's arm and places it around Eve, and puts these words in his mouth: "But rise, let us no more contend, nor blame each other, blam'd enough elsewhere, but strive in offices of Love, how we may light'n each others burden in our share of woe."[3] I've read Emily Dickinson the playful and poignant poet: "I'm Nobody! Who are you? Are you— Nobody—too?"[4] I've watched Captain Ahab relentlessly pursue the white whale.

And I've read the parchments by Paul himself, where he tells us: "Finally, brothers, whatever is true, whatever is honorable, whatever is just, whatever is pure, whatever is lovely, whatever is commendable, if there is any excellence, if there is anything worthy of praise, think about these things" (Phil. 4:8). Books help us do that. They lay out for us the whole breadth of the human condition, reflect the best of man's creative work as God's image bearer, and point out our need for a Savior, to the glory of God.

EPILOGUE

THE NEXT FIVE HUNDRED YEARS: A CONVERSATION WITH R.C. SPROUL

SN: For our two hundredth episode of *5 Minutes in Church History*, we have a very special guest, Dr. R.C. Sproul. Welcome back.

RS: Thank you very much, Steve. It's a delight to be with you.

SN: Well, not only are we celebrating the two hundredth installment, it happens to fall in the year 2017. Now, why is this an important year, Dr. Sproul?

RS: It's the five hundredth anniversary of the Protestant Reformation as dated from Martin Luther's posting of the Ninety-Five Theses at the church door at Wittenberg.

SN: As you stop and think about that moment—and I know it's a moment you've thought about often—you cannot overestimate the value of what happened on October 31, 1517.

RS: I quite agree on that. That's a watershed moment in the history of the church.

SN: As you think of Luther and his influence not only on the church, but even on Western history and culture, tell us about the influence of Luther in your own life.

RS: When I became a Christian in a sudden conversion in my freshman year of college, I assumed and adopted the basic, standard Arminian position on theology. Roger Nicole used to say that we were by nature Pelagian in our thinking. And it wasn't until I really started studying the Reformers that I came to an understanding of the doctrines of grace and really understood justification by faith alone. Now, obviously, as a new convert I had no concept of theology. I wasn't involved in debates about the how and the why and the where of justification; I just knew I was a sinner who had been forgiven of his sin. But when I began to study the doctrine of *sola fide*—justification by faith alone—which was so central to Luther's protest, then my eyes were opened and I realized, yes, this is exactly what happened to me. I didn't do anything to earn it; I didn't do anything to achieve it. It was solely by the grace of God.

SN: I've heard you refer many times to the last sermon that Luther preached at Wittenberg. In that sermon, Luther gives a stern warning to his congregation about this very doctrine and its place and its prominence in the life of the church.

RS: Yes, he said that in every generation, the gospel has to be understood anew; it has to be preached with vigor and urgency, because as quickly as we receive it and understand it, like the ancient Galatians, we are fast to move away from it and try to interject some additive that we give to secure our own justification. It is always faith plus something rather than faith alone.

SN: We smuggle in works.

RS: Yes, we do.

SN: Paul warned Timothy, "Guard the good deposit."[1] That is why we study church history: to remind us of these men God raised up to guard that good deposit, and that's even the task in our own day. We continue this great legacy we've been handed and guard the good deposit of faith.

RS: Yes indeed.

SN: Dr. Sproul, I'd like to thank you for joining us on this occasion as we step back in time and remember our good friend Martin Luther and how God used him to bring about reformation in the church. Five hundred years later, we are still enjoying the benefits and the fruits of his labors. We only pray that God would use this current generation to make its mark, so that five hundred years from now we might be talking about the legacy that the church of today leaves behind.

RS: I sure hope so.

NOTES

Chapter 1

1   C.H. Spurgeon, *Commenting and Commentaries: A Reference Guide to the Best Bible Study Books* (Grand Rapids, Mich.: Kregel, 1988), 13, emphasis original.

Chapter 2

1   Ignatius, "The Epistle to the Ephesians," "Early Christian Writings: New Testament, Apocrypha, Gnostics, Church Fathers." *Early Christian Writings*. Accessed July 3, 2018. http://www.earlychristianwritings.com.

2   Ignatius, "The Epistle of Ignatius to the Smyrnaeans," *Early Christian Writings*.

3   Ignatius, "The Epistle of Ignatius to the Smyrnaeans," *Early Christian Writings*.

4   Pliny the Younger, "Pliny the Younger to the Emperor Trajan," *Early Christian Writings*.

Chapter 3

1   Michael W. Holmes, *The Apostolic Fathers in English* (Grand Rapids, Mich.: Baker Academic, 2006), 150.

2   Holmes, 150.

3   Holmes, 155.

Chapter 4

1   Eusebius, *Church History*, vol. 1, *Nicene and Post-Nicene Fathers of the Christian Church*, eds. Philip Schaff and Henry Wace, trans. Arthur Cushman McGiffert (Grand Rapids, Mich.: Eerdmans, 1982), 5.1.19.

2   Eusebius, *Church History*, 5.1.19.

3   Eusebius, *Church History*, 5.1.19.

4   Eusebius, *Church History*, 5.1.19.

5   Eusebius, *Church History*, 5.1.19.

Chapter 5

1 Vincenzo Fiocchi Nicolai, Fabrizio Bisconti, and Danilo Mazzoleni, *The Christian Catacombs of Rome: History, Decoration, Inscriptions* (Regensburg, Germany: Schnell & Steiner, 2002), 172.
2 Nicolai, Bisconti, and Mazzoleni, 172.
3 Nicolai, Bisconti, and Mazzoleni, 173.
4 Nicolai, Bisconti, and Mazzoleni, 173.
5 Nicolai, Bisconti, and Mazzoleni, 174.
6 Nicolai, Bisconti, and Mazzoleni, 174.

Chapter 7

1 *Annals of Tacitus*, trans. Alfred Church and William Brodribb (Pennsylvania: The Franklin Library, 1982), 344.

Chapter 9

1 Augustine, *Confessions*, trans. Garry Wills (New York: Penguin, 2006), 3.
2 Augustine, *Confessions*, trans. Rex Warner (Springdale, Pa.: Whitaker House, 1996), 11.
3 Alister E. McGrath, *The Christian Theology Reader* (Oxford, England: Blackwell, 1998), 218.

Chapter 11

1 Geoffrey Chaucer, *Canterbury Tales: A Selection,* ed. J.U. Nicolson (Ann Arbor, Mich.: Borders, 2007), 3.

Chapter 13

1 Ellis J. Crum, "He Paid a Debt He Did Not Owe," 1977.

Chapter 14

1 Aristotle, *Metaphysics*, trans. Hugh Lawson-Tancred (London: Penguin, 2004), 12.1072b.
2 Thomas Aquinas, *Summa Theologiae Prima Pars*, 1–49/Saint Thomas Aquinas, ed. John Mortensen, Enrique Alarcón, trans. Laurence Shapcote (Steubenville, Ohio: Emmaus Academic, 2012), 23.
3 Aquinas, 37–41.
4 Aquinas, 39.

Chapter 18

1 Scott H. Hendrix, *Martin Luther: Visionary Reformer* (New Haven, Conn.: Yale University Press, 2015), 24.
2 Roland H. Bainton, *Here I Stand: A Life of Martin Luther* (New York: Plume, 1995), 15.

3 Bainton, *Here I Stand*, 34.

4 Bainton, *Here I Stand*, 38.

Chapter 19

1 Martin Luther, *Martin Luther's Ninety-Five Theses*, ed. Stephen J. Nichols (Phillipsburg, N.J.: P&R, 2002), 23.

2 Luther, *Ninety-Five Theses*, 23.

3 Luther, *Ninety-Five Theses*, 23.

Chapter 20

1 William H. Lazareth, *Luther on the Christian Home: An Application of the Social Ethics of the Reformation* (Philadelphia: Muhlenberg, 1960), 7.

2 Roland H. Bainton, *Women of the Reformation in Germany and Italy* (Minneapolis, Minn.: Fortress, 2007), 26.

3 Bainton, *Women of the Reformation in Germany and Italy*, 42.

Chapter 21

1 J.H. Merle d'Aubigné, *The Reformation in England*, vol. 2, ed. S.M. Houghton (Edinburgh, Scotland: Banner of Truth, 2015), 347.

2 D'Aubigné, *The Reformation in England*, 2:351.

3 D'Aubigné, *The Reformation in England*, 2:351.

Chapter 22

1 Martin Luther, *Luther's Works*, eds. Ulrich S. Leupold and Helmut T. Lehmann (Philadelphia: Fortress, 1984), 53:323.

2 Martin Luther, *The Annotated Luther*, ed. Mary Jane Haemig (Minneapolis, Minn.: Fortress, 2016), 4:105.

Chapter 23

1 James T. Dennison, *Reformed Confessions of the 16th and 17th Centuries in English Translation*, vol. 2, *1552–1566* (Grand Rapids, Mich.: Reformation Heritage, 2010), 465.

2 Dennison, *Reformed Confessions*, 2:465.

3 Dennison, *Reformed Confessions*, 2:466.

4 Dennison, *Reformed Confessions*, 2:466.

5 Dennison, *Reformed Confessions*, 2:466.

Chapter 24

1 John Calvin to Pierre Viret, Ulm, March 1, 1541, *Letters of John Calvin*, trans. D. Constable, ed. Jules Bonnet (Philadelphia: Presbyterian Board of Publication, 1858), 1.231.

2   Jean-François Gilmont, *John Calvin and the Printed Book*, trans. Karin Maag (Kirksville, Mo.: Truman State University Press, 2005), 4.

3   Gilmont, 4.

Chapter 25

1   Dennison, *Reformed Confessions*, 2:118.

2   Dennison, *Reformed Confessions*, 2:122.

3   Dennison, *Reformed Confessions*, 2:123.

4   Dennison, *Reformed Confessions*, 2:124.

Chapter 26

1   Albert Bushnell, *American History Told by Contemporaries*, vol. 1 (New York: Macmillan, 1908), 114.

Chapter 27

1   William Shakespeare, *Richard II*, ed. Nigel Saul (New Haven, Conn.: Yale University Press, 1999). 1.1.174–75.

2   Naseeb Shaheen, *Biblical References in Shakespeare's Plays* (Newark, Del.: University of Delaware Press, 2002), 363.

3   Shakespeare, *Richard II*, 1.3.202.

4   Shaheen, *Biblical References*, 367.

5   William Shakespeare, *As You Like It*, ed. S.C. Burchell (New Haven, Conn.: Yale University Press, 1965), 3.2.129–31.

6   William Shakespeare, *The Life of Timon of Athens*, ed. Stanley T. Williams (New Haven, Conn.: Yale University Press, 1919), 5.1.165–66.

Chapter 28

1   John D. Woodbridge and Frank A. James, *Church History: The Rise and Growth of the Church in Its Cultural, Intellectual, and Political Context*, vol. 2 (Grand Rapids, Mich.: Zondervan, 2013), 265.

2   Woodbridge and James, *Church History*, 2:267.

Chapter 29

1   William Ames, *The Marrow of Theology*, trans. John Dykstra Eusden (Grand Rapids, Mich.: Baker, 1997), 77.

2   Ames, 78.

Chapter 30

1   Daniel Defoe, *Robinson Crusoe*, ed. John Mullan (New York: A.A. Knopf, 1992), 67.

2   Defoe, *Robinson Crusoe*, 80.

Chapter 31

1   *The Works of Jonathan Edwards*, vol. 16, *Letters and Personal Writings*, ed. George S. Claghorn (New Haven, Conn.: Yale University Press, 1998), 792.

2   *The Works of Jonathan Edwards*, vol. 17, *Sermons and Discourses, 1730–1733*, ed. Mark Valeri (New Haven, Conn.: Yale University Press, 1999), 208.

Chapter 32

1   *The Works of Jonathan Edwards*, vol. 7, eds. Norman Pettit, Perry Miller, John E. Smith, and Harry S. Stout (New Haven, Conn.: Yale University Press, 1985), 139.

2   *The Works of Johathan Edwards*, 7:155.

Chapter 33

1   Thabiti M. Anyabwile, *The Faithful Preacher: Recapturing the Vision of Three Pioneering African-American Pastors* (Wheaton, Ill.: Crossway, 2007), 28–29.

Chapter 34

1   *The Autobiography of Benjamin Franklin* (United States: Millennium Publications, 2015), 70.

2   *Autobiography of Benjamin Franklin*, 70.

3   William Cabell Bruce, *Benjamin Franklin Self-Revealed*, vol. 1 (New York: G.P. Putnam's Sons, 1917), 78.

4   *Autobiography of Benjamin Franklin*, 71.

5   *Autobiography of Benjamin Franklin*, 71.

Chapter 35

1   Mark Sidwell, *Free Indeed: Heroes of Black Christian History* (Greenville, S.C.: BJU Press, 2001), 122.

2   Sidwell, *Free Indeed*, 127.

Chapter 36

1   O.T. Allis, "Personal Impressions of Dr. Warfield," *Banner of Truth* 89 (Fall 1971): 10–14.

2   Ned Stonehouse, *J. Gresham Machen: A Biographical Memoir* (Grand Rapids, Mich.: Eerdmans, 1954), 309–10.

3   Stonehouse, *J. Gresham Machen*, 220.

Chapter 37

1   J. Gresham Machen, "Mountains and Why We Love Them," *Christianity Today*, August 1934: 66–68.

2 Machen, "Mountains and Why We Love Them."

3 Machen, "Mountains and Why We Love Them."

4 Machen, "Mountains and Why We Love Them."

Chapter 38

1 Machen Archives, Westminster Theological Seminary, Philadelphia, April 7, 1917.

2 J. Gresham Machen, *Letters from the Front: J. Gresham Machen's Correspondence from World War I*, ed. Barry G. Waugh (Philadelphia: Westminster Seminary Press, 2012), 92.

3 Machen, *Letters from the Front*, 74.

4 Machen, *Letters from the Front*, 134.

5 Machen, *Letters from the Front*, 213.

6 Machen, *Letters from the Front*, 215.

Chapter 39

1 Simon Burton, "Eulogy of Eric Liddell," *The Guardian*, May 11, 1945.

Chapter 40

1 John Calvin, *Calvin's Commentaries*, vol. 21, *The Epistles of Paul to the Galatians, Ephesians, Philippians, Colossians, I & II Thess., I & II Timothy, Titus, Philemon* (Grand Rapids, Mich.: Baker, 2005), 266.

2 Neil Postman, *Amusing Ourselves to Death: Public Discourse in the Age of Show Business* (New York: Penguin, 2006).

3 John Milton, *Paradise Lost*, ed. Barbara K. Lewalski (Malden, Mass.: Blackwell, 2008), 279.

4 *The Complete Poems of Emily Dickinson*, ed. Thomas Herbert Johnson (Boston: Little, Brown, 2015), 288.

Epilogue

1 2 Timothy 1:14.

SUBJECT INDEX

ABOUT THE AUTHOR

Dr. Stephen J. Nichols is president of Reformation Bible College in Sanford, Fla., and chief academic officer and a teaching fellow for Ligonier Ministries. He earned his Ph.D. from Westminster Theological Seminary and earned master's degrees from West Chester University in Pennsylvania and Westminster Theological Seminary.

Dr. Nichols is a prolific writer who has written, contributed to, or edited more than thirty books on church history, biblical doctrine, and practical theology. Among his books are *For Us and for Our Salvation, Jesus Made in America, Martin Luther: A Guided Tour of His Life and Thought, Heaven on Earth: Capturing Jonathan Edwards's Vision of Living in Between, The Reformation*, and *Peace*. He is also the coeditor for the Theologians on the Christian Life series from Crossway, and he hosts the podcasts *Open Book* and *5 Minutes in Church History*.